IMAGES OF ST

Figure Sculpture of the Lough Ern

R. Jack

IMAGES OF STONE

HELEN HICKEY

Photographs by Bill Porter

Blackstaff Press

Published in association with the Arts Council of Northern Ireland by Blackstaff Press Limited, 16 Donegall Square South, Belfast BT1 5JF.

ISBN 0 85640 110 2

Printed by Belfast Litho Printers Limited.

Contents

Acknowledgements

It is a pleasure to acknowledge the help of so many in the production of this book and the accompanying exhibition:- Dudley Waterman, Inspector of Historic Monuments for much helpful advice and for allowing me to use material collected during my archaeological survey work in Fermanagh; the Director and staff of the Arts Council of Northern Ireland, in particular Brian Ferran; the Director and staff of the Ulster Museum, Larry McCandless and Alan Campbell for making such skilful casts for the exhibition, Bill Porter, Nancy Ferguson, Lawrence Flanagan, Richard Warner, Winifred Glover, Tom Delaney, Pamela Tricker, Brian Turner, Wendy Osborne, Tony Eveleigh, Adrienne Anderson and in particular Ted Hickey for his encouragement and helpful comments; the Director and staff of the National Museum, Dublin, in particular Dr Joseph Raftery for providing casts and photographs p 32, 35 and 63 and nos 1, 2, 4, 8, 38, 50 and 51; Mary Rogers, Thomas Barron, Katherine Simms, Patrick Cassidy, Tom McCabe, Anthony Weir, Ann Hamlin, Hugh Dixon, Jack O'Brien, Vincent Mahon, Rev K E Ruddock, Rev J R Sides, Malcolm Fry, William Shannon, T P Flanagan, Seamus Heaney and Diane Gracey. Finally I would like to record my debt to my former teacher Dr Françoise Henry whose scholarly work is a continual source of inspiration.

Exhibits were kindly lent by the Archaeological Survey, Belfast, the Fermanagh District Council, Mount Lourdes Convent of Mercy, Enniskillen, John Barron, Patrick Cassidy and Mr & Mrs Ritchie. W Surphlis, Frank Blake and Douglas Roe kindly allowed casts to be made of their carvings.

For permission to reproduce photographs we acknowledge the courtesy of the Photographic Archives, Department of Archaeology, University College, Dublin for p 38; The Master and Fellows of St John's College, Cambridge for p 47; La Conservation des Musees d'Archeologie, Chateau Borely, Marseilles for p 15; the Office of Public Works, Dublin for the Carndonagh Pillar on p 35; Thomas Barron for no 5; Ann Hamlin for no 17; the Ulster Museum for nos 14, 15, 26 and 28 by R J Welch; Nancy Ferguson for no 40; the Archaeological Survey, Belfast for no 16 by Helen Hickey; nos 12, 15, 25, 43, 52, 53 and 60 were also by Helen Hickey. The drawings of nos 7, 20 and 33 are by Deirdre Crone; the maps were drawn by Gillian Sands. For permission to quote from *Pagan Celtic Britain* by Anne Ross we thank Routledge and Kegan Paul, London and Columbia University Press, New York.

Introduction

Many authorities on Early Christian (5th-12th century AD) and Romanesque (12th century AD) art in Ireland have remarked on how earlier 'Celtic' (3rd century BC - 5th century AD) traditions of figure-carving seem to linger on to affect the work of later stone-carvers. The Christian statues on White Island in Fermanagh, for example, are thought to retain features characteristic of Pagan idols from the same area.[1] The popularity of the human head motif on Romanesque arches finds its analogy in 'Celtic' head-carvings.[2] This regional survey of figure-sculpture has revealed a remarkable archaism among the stone-carvers of the Lough Erne area, evident not only during the Early Christian and Romanesque periods, as occurs in other parts of Ireland, but strongly persistent throughout Medieval times (13th-16th century AD) and down to the 19th and 20th century.

Archaism

This enduring archaism may be explained to some extent by the geographical isolation of Cavan and Fermanagh which would tend to discourage the influx of vigorous new populations into the area. The absence of Norman settlement certainly played a part in the conservatism apparent in the Medieval period. Some significance may also be attached to the fact that the traditions which persisted most strongly were those originally associated with the Pagan religion.

The widespread persistence of Pagan traditions in folklore, Christianity and early Irish literature has long been recognized. Indeed some contemporary devotions such as the veneration of the head of St Oliver Plunket in Drogheda could be regarded as survivals from pre-Christian cult practices. Another devotion recorded in Cavan in the 17th century certainly smacks of idolatry! This took place near Urney Church and consisted of the veneration of the carved head of St Brigid set in a heap of stones.[3] If Pagan traditions persisted in these areas it is not surprising to find them reflected in sculpture as well.

This archaistic tendency among the Lough Erne stonecarvers often leads to difficulties in dating their work accurately. Medieval head carvings frequently resemble those of the Romanesque period but can usually be dated by their architectural associations. It is not so easy to date examples of Post-Medieval folk-art and there are at least two carvings tentatively claimed as Post-Medieval which would not be out of place among 'Celtic' idols carved perhaps two thousand years earlier! The most recent head is made of concrete. Had it been made of stone a much earlier date for it would have been acceptable. This illustrates most vividly a fact which is beginning to be generally recognized — that many simply carved heads of different dates are essentially similar. The difficulties of dating isolated stone heads are not confined to the Lough Erne area nor indeed to Ireland. Recently a Romanesque date has been argued for the well-known carved head from Gloucester which used to be regarded as one of the best examples of Romano-Celtic sculpture in Britain![4]

Although this sculpture has been studied mainly from an archaeological viewpoint it is hoped that this illustrated publication and the exhibition accompanying it[5] will lead to a more general appreciation of these figure-carvings as works of art. And just as Henry Moore derived the basic impulse for his images from his discovery of Mexican art of the Pre-Columban period so perhaps will sculptors and artists be drawn to these carvings for their inspirational qualities.

Idols of the Celtic Religion

3rd century BC to 5th century AD

JANUARY GOD

Then I found a two-faced stone
On burial ground,
God-eyed, sex-mouthed, its brain
A watery wound.

In the wet gap of the year,
Daubed with fresh lake mud,
I faltered near his power —
January god

Who broke the water, the hymen
With his great antlers —
There reigned upon each ghost tine
His familiars,

The mothering earth, the stones
Taken by each wave,
The fleshy aftergrass, the bones
Subsoil in each grave.

Seamus Heaney

Origin of Celts

The original home of the Celts was in central Europe in Bohemia and Bavaria. In that area during the first milennium BC prosperous tribes emerged using iron tools and weapons. They traded salt and probably slaves with the mediterranean world in exchange for such luxury goods as wine imported along with beautifully fashioned bronze vessels. From central Europe these people spread as far east as Asia Minor, as far west as Ireland. Their surviving place-names and river-names indicate that they spoke closely related dialects which have been called 'Celtic' by linguists. This 'Celtic' language had separated from the parent Indo-European as early as 2,000 BC.[1] Despite regional differences the new art forms created by these widely scattered peoples are also remarkably similar.

'Celtic' Art and Religion

The mature form of this art, known as La Tène, appears in Ireland during the Early Iron Age, from about the 3rd century BC. When archaeologists in Ireland use the term 'Celtic' they are referring to the patterns of material culture of this period before the introduction of Christianity. For want of better, we continue here to use this much misused term as including in its terms of reference the art and religion of the period.

The most evocative physical remains of the 'Celtic' religion in Ireland are stone pillars and idols. The pillars are phallic-shaped, either plain as at Killadeas in Fermanagh or richly decorated with curvilinear patterns as at Killycluggin in Cavan, or Turoe in Galway. The idols occur in a variety of forms and are widely distributed in Ulster. The Lough Erne area is particularly rich in such figures as is Armagh, where the site of an important 'Celtic' sanctuary has been identified on Cathedral hill. These idols are now weathered and often placed in incongruous surroundings far removed from the temples in which they were originally revered. Yet they still retain about them a strange power and aura. The poem 'January God' by Seamus Heaney has as its subject the two-faced idol from Boa Island in Fermanagh, and subtly conveys the sense of wonder and mystery evoked by these strange carvings, so inaccessible in their stony dignity to present day consciousness.

Apart from archaeology, the other main sources for our knowledge of 'Celtic' religion are the observations of Greek and Roman writers and the early literature of Ireland and Wales. The difficulties of interpreting this information have often been pointed out. The classical references are generally to the religious practices of the continental Celts and need not necessarily apply to Irish customs. However, frequently there is a remarkable accord between the evidence from all three sources enabling us to understand, at least in general terms, some of the religious ideas of these people.

The Cult of the Human Head

The most important 'Celtic' religious symbol was the human head which was seen as the pre-eminent symbol of divinity and supernatural power. It was common throughout the entire Celtic world and seems to have had much the same importance and emblematic significance in 'Celtic' religion as the cross was to have in Christianity. In earlier cults in Bronze Age Europe the human head was sometimes used as a sun symbol while in Etruscan art the carved head was used as a symbol for the whole warrior.[2] The 'Celtic' idea of the isolated head as a potent symbol probably owes much to traditions such as these.

The cult of the carved head also appears to be connected with a reverence for severed human heads. The most illuminating archaeological evidence for this comes from a number of 'Celtic' sanctuaries in the Provence area of southern France, not far from the early Greek colony centred at Massalia (present day Marseilles). The monumental architectural qualities of these sanctuaries deriving from classical traditions distinguishes them from the more widespread type of 'Celtic' sanctuary further north, which consisted of enclosed sanctuary areas and small timber temples.[3] Architectural details in stone have survived in Provence, in particular from the sanctuaries in Entremont, in the oppidum of Salyens (the Saluvii), and from Roquepertuse also within an oppidum enclosure. The timber temples, on the other hand, have been totally destroyed, and only their foundations can be traced by excavation.

The Head Cult in Provence

A lintel from a portico at Entremont, belonging to the 3rd or 2nd century BC, contained a carving of a human head within a small recess. On either side of it were two empty niches, almost certainly designed to hold embalmed human skulls. The opposite face of the lintel also contained two skull-niches, more roughly carved. Skulls were also found on the site — in all twenty decapitated skulls — some cut from dried bodies, some with iron nails attached.[4] It is quite remarkable to find such strong archaeological evidence for this remote cult. Even stranger cults were practised here. Among the many carvings of human heads from the site were six each with a large hand grasping the top of the head. These point to a particularly mysterious practice, probably confined to this locality, of which the most horrific expression is seen in a statue from another 'Celtic' sanctuary at Noves, also in Provence. This is the famous statue of a monster grasping a human head in each paw while devouring a human hand.[5]

The sanctuary at Roquepertuse, probably built in the 4th century BC, also had a portico containing skull niches. All the decapitated heads from the site were found to be male, none more than forty years of age. Since there is evidence that the temple was dedicated to the local god of war it has been very plausibly suggested that these skulls were those of prized enemies taken in the prime of life, a view corroborated by Livy's description of how the 'Celtic' Boii tribe sacrificed prisoners.[6]

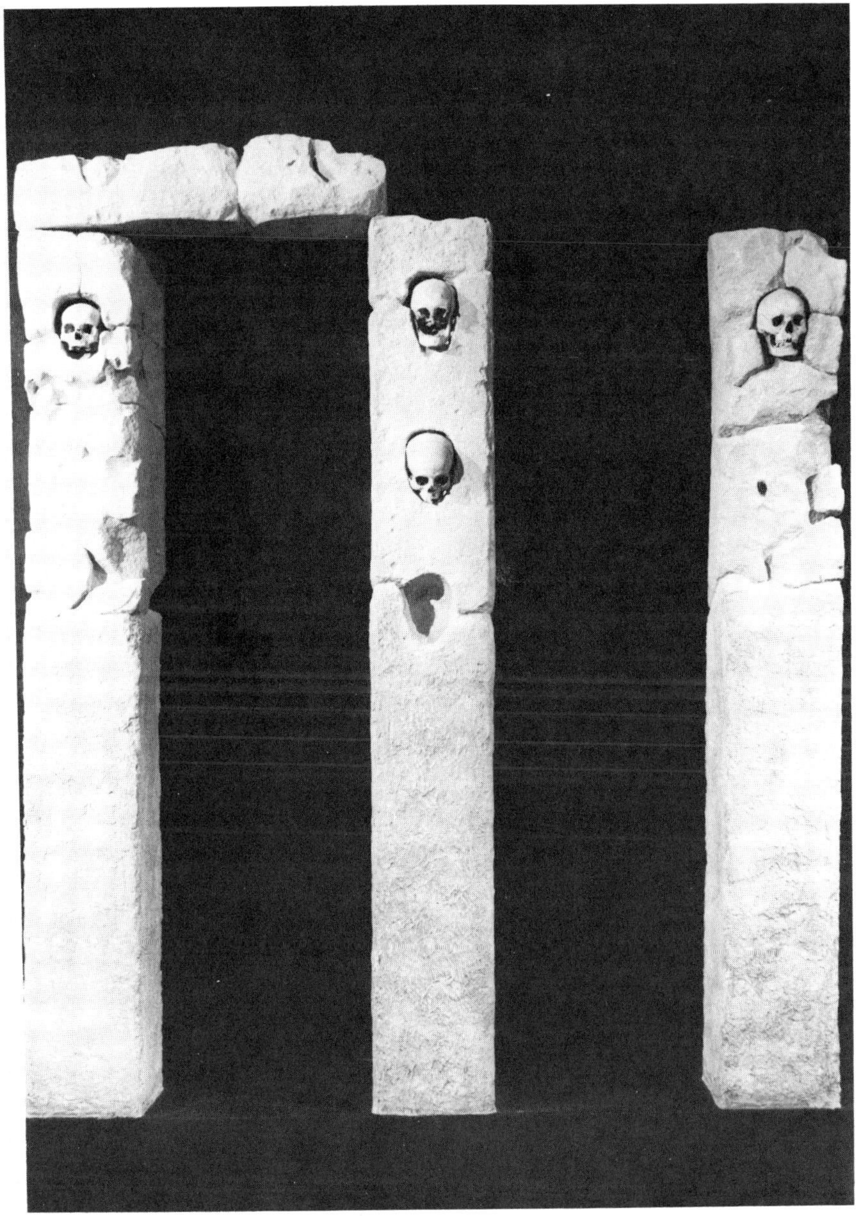

Portico at Roquepertuse

The Head Cult in Ireland

The custom of taking the heads of slain enemies was practised in Ireland as well as in Gaul. There are numerous references in the early Irish sagas to the return of heroes from battle bearing the heads of their enemies and subsequently displaying them in front of their houses. There are also historical references to this practice including one from Co. Fermanagh in 1185 when the severed head of Gilla Crist Mac Cathmhail, Royal chief of Cenel Feradhaigh was carried away by his killers and kept for a month.[7] Myles Dillon suggests that 'the head may have been thought to contain the spirit after death, and possession of the head prolonged the triumph of the slayer.'[8] A version of a folk tale about Balor and Lugh certainly seems to embody a belief that the severed head retains its power and efficacy.[9] The tale recounts that Balor asks Lugh to behead him and to put the head on top of his own so that he may get Balor's power. In this instance Lugh, suspecting Balor of evil intent, puts the head on a rock which is split by its venom. A more straightforward explanation of the practice of displaying enemies' heads is that they were simply intended as a deterrent to intimidate and demoralize the enemy. This was common practice by the English in medieval Ireland following confrontations with insurgents. During the same period the native Fermanagh chieftain Thomas Óg Maguire was celebrating his victory over the O'Rourkes in 1457 ('Annals of Ulster') by adorning the posts of his garden with the heads of sixteen of his enemies.

That heads of Kings and heroes were also preserved and honoured is clear from references in Welsh and Irish tales. There is a very interesting reference in the Irish saga 'The Battle of Allen' to the head of the warrior, Donn Bo, being set upon a pillar after the battle, when it sings forth to the Leinstermen.[10] Speaking heads are also mentioned in Welsh literature. These references hint at a ritual ceremony involving the slain head in an oracular capacity.

Two heads from Co. Cavan look like carved representations of severed human heads, one from Corravilla, the other from near Cavan town. The lintel from Entremont with its combination of skull niches and carved head clearly illustrates the religious connection between the cult of the embalmed skull in Provence and that of its sculptural manifestation. Lacking this kind of evidence in Ireland we can only speculate on the meaning and function of the Cavan heads. If they were, as seems probable, a sort of permanent commemoration of the human skull, they are more likely to represent slain heroes than slain enemies. Their less esoteric functions probably included that of averting evil and bringing good luck. Another possibility is that they formed part of a fertility cult and were perhaps set upon a sone pillar to serve as a phallic symbol. There is strong evidence that heads were used for this purpose in Britain and on the Continent,[11] although the fact that only the facial area of the Cavan heads were carved makes this explanation less likely.

Other Cults

The Two-faced God

The double figure from Boa Island in Fermanagh is a cult idol of very complex origins. Although it now stands in a Christian graveyard it is certainly not an early Christian statue as some writers have suggested. Its four salient features — the janus form (Janus strictly means a two-faced figure but can refer to two figures or heads back to back) the phallus shown on one side, the belt and the crossed limbs — have striking parallels in the 'Celtic' iconography of Britain and the Continent.

There were undoubtedly very complicated religious reasons for depicting this God as a two-faced one. The double form could reflect the 'Celtic' belief in the power of twins who, it was believed, enjoyed special divine protection.[12] It could also reflect a primitive belief that in duplicating features one was in some way intensifying the power of the idol.[13] It could suggest as well that the cult on Boa Island resembled the Roman cult of Janus.

It is not usual for the phallus to be represented on 'Celtic' idols. An exception is the early stone statue from Hirschlanden in Germany[14] where the unexaggerated treatment of the organ compares with the Fermanagh figure. In determining the male nature of the idol this feature rules out the theory that the Boa Island figure was connected with Badhbh, (Irish Raven or Hooded Crow) Goddess of War, from which the name Boa is said to derive. It suggests that the promotion of fertility was one of the functions of this idol, a function more usually attributed to the phallic shaped pillar stones of this period.

A belt is very frequently shown on Celtic stone idols including the statue already referred to from Hirschlanden and the well known janiform figure from Holzgerlingen also in Germany. Like the torque so often depicted on these idols the belt must have been a symbolic emblem of the god-hero, perhaps related to its practical function of holding weapons and possibly skull trophies.

The strangely positioned limbs of the Boa Island idol are usually taken to be crossed arms, protruding as they do from shoulder level. However the end of one limb looks very like a foot suggesting that one side at least was meant to illustrate squatting legs — the so-called Buddhic posture. 'Celtic' idols are commonly shown in this position in Central France[15] and these squatting gods are frequently but not always accompanied by the attributes of the stag-god Cernunnos, notably antlers. Some writers have described the Boa Island idol as a horned god but neither Rynne nor I could find any evidence for vestigial horns. If the limbs on one of its sides are in fact legs and if those on the opposite side above the phallus are arms, then the idol would be strictly janiform — a two-faced god with all the essential attributes of a single body. The 'Buddhic pose' is supposed to indicate oriental influence in 'Celtic' religion. On the other hand it may be nothing more mysterious than a representation of the normal sitting posture of the Celts who, according to classical writers, never used chairs!

Another very interesting feature of the Boa Island idol is the hollow in the top surface of the stone. Perhaps, as several writers have suggested,[16] it was a hollow to contain drink or blood offerings to the god. Alternatively it could be a socket designed to hold a leaf crown in stone,[17] which was one of the 'Celtic' insignia of divinity, or perhaps a carving of the branched horns of a stag. Both of these types of head-gear are frequently shown on 'Celtic' idols from France and Germany and a particularly fine example of the antlered crown occurs on the famous Gundestrup cauldron from Denmark, on a deity seated in the Buddhic posture.

Few writers have commented on the linear pattern carved on one of the narrow sides of the stone, between the two heads. It could easily be mistaken for interlacing on account of the weathered nature of the stone, but a close examination reveals that only one strand crosses over another, hardly enough for one to accept the pattern as the earliest example of Irish interlacing! It may represent hair although in that case one would expect a similar pattern on the opposite side. However the same pattern is used to represent a beard on a carved three-faced 'Celtic' deity from Reims in France.[18]

The Three-faced God

The three-faced head from Corleck in Cavan, well known for the simplicity and beauty of its sculptural form, is remarkable too as an expression of yet another religious idea of the Celts. While three-faced stone heads are rare in Britain and Ireland, references from the early Irish tales make it clear that the number three had a special magico-religious significance for the pagan Irish. Anne Ross in *Pagan Celtic Britain*[19] comments that these tales 'contain references to three semi-divine heroes rather than one, born at a single birth, and being given the same name, but distinguishing epithets . . . deities are grouped in threes; the traditional lore of both Wales and Ireland is preserved in a series of triadic statements, and this predilection for the number three can be discerned throughout the Celtic tradition'. There is some evidence to suggest that the worship of three-faced gods, if not confined to particular 'Celtic' tribes, was at least more popular in certain regions than in others. It was for example particularly widespread in the territory of certain Belgic 'Celtic' tribes known as Remi in northern France. Richard Warner has also observed that in the Irish saga, the 'Táin Bó Cúailgne', the triadic element is confined to the Connacht side and the Ulster god-heroes are always single.

Role of the Corleck God

The Corleck god may be much earlier than the three-faced gods of the Remi, which belong to the Gallo-Roman period, but perhaps it played a similar role. The triadic Gaulish gods were equated by the Remi with the Roman god Mercury[20] which suggests that at least some of the functions of their gods must have compared with those of the Roman god. But we know that the 'Celtic' deities played far more varied and complex roles than the Roman gods. The different cults overlapped to a large extent and there were no rigid divisions between the areas controlled by each god. So the most that we can suggest from the link with the Roman god is that the Corleck god, like Mercury, was concerned with all aspects of human and animal fecundity, with protecting the herds and flocks and maintaining prosperity among the tribe. One cannot be sure that the triplication of the face was intended to represent a particularly powerful god[21] but it does suggest that the Corleck god was regarded as being all-seeing.

An unusual feature on one of the Corleck faces is the small hole cut in the centre of the mouth. The significance of this has never been explained. It occurs on other tricephalic idols as well as on single heads in Britain and on the Continent.[22] Was it to release the spirit of the idol and allow its beneficial properties to act? Was it to suggest a musical sound such as whistling or chanting emitted as part of a religious or oracular ritual? Or was it simply to suggest the emission of oracular speech?

Double Idol of Human and Ram's Head

An interesting new discovery in Irish archaeology is that the stone head from Corraghy, about two miles from Corleck, was part of a double idol originally combined with the head of a ram. For a period of about ten years in the middle of the 19th century this janiform carving, then complete, was displayed with the tricephalic Corleck head and the head from Corravilla on a wall in front of a house in Corleck. According to local information the Corleck head was set directly on top of the janiform human-cum-ram idol.

Controversial Theory

Thomas Barron of Bailieboro in Cavan, who discovered and identified the surviving portion of the janiform carving, believes that these two idols were originally grouped in this manner and worshipped as a 'Celtic' pantheon.[23] Iconographic associations between three-faced gods and the ram are known, the most significant links being with the tricephalic god of the Remi in northern France.[24] The Corleck head contains a small hole in its base evidently for attaching it to a pedestal. Only if a corresponding tenon had survived in the human-cum-ram idol would there be enough evidence for accepting Mr. Barron's theory.

The Religious Significance of the Human cum Ram Idol

The conjunction of a human head with that of a beast as a religious image certainly requires some explanation. Its meaning is far from clear. Some would see it as marking a transition between a primitive worship of the animal itself and a more evolved type of religion where the deity takes on human form. This however is no more than an attractive hypothesis as no proof exists that the Celts ever worshipped animals as such. In primitive religions animals sometimes became deified because they were regarded as having superior god-like qualities which contrasted sharply with the weaknesses and imperfections of human nature. By linking the animal image with the human head the intention may have been to imbue the Cavan deity with the god-like qualities of the ram, fertility, no doubt, being included as one of these!

My own view is that the religious significance of the animal on this idol derived from the undoubted importance of the ram in the economic life of the Cavan community. The part of Cavan in which it was found is mostly rough pasture best suited to sheep farming. The association of the ram's head with the smiling human head must surely reflect the deity's involvement with the well-being and fertility of the flock. A similar explanation could account for certain continental 'Celtic' deities being shown with ram's horns, and perhaps for the ram's head being frequently associated with a human head on continental La Tène metalwork.

Similar Idol in Yorkshire

The only other idol comparable with the Corraghy carving was found ten years ago built into a wall in Mirfield, Yorkshire.[25] The reconstruction of the Cavan idol is based on this example. From the similarity of these two idols one could argue that the tribes of Cavan and Yorkshire held similar religious beliefs, perhaps the result of a common continental ancestry. Had the Cavan ram survived it might even have been possible to argue, on the basis of close stylistic comparisons between the two idols, in favour of direct links between the peoples of Cavan and Yorkshire.

No trace remains of the sanctuary in which the Corleck three-faced god and this human-cum-ram idol were worshipped. A tempting and attractive suggestion is that it was sited on Corleck Hill, where a Lúnasa festival, originally in honour of the god Lugh, continued to be observed as a peasant festive assembly until c. 1831.[26] The peasant festival was held in honour of three saints, thought to be Patrick, Brigid and Columcille. It does not seem too fanciful to regard this dedication as marking a Christian takeover of a pagan cult associated with the veneration of a three-faced god.

The two remaining stone carvings were found on Christian sites, one from the graveyard on Lustymore Island in Fermanagh, the other from the vicinity of a chapel well in Enniskillen. The former is probably a pagan idol related to the Boa Island idol beside which it now stands. The fact that only one eye is fully carved may be of significance, indicating perhaps that the other eye — the left eye — is blind. In early Irish tales Cu Chulainn has more than one encounter with divine hags who are described as blind in the left eye. These hags or crones are believed to be manifestations of war-goddesses.[27]

The Enniskillen carving, now in Irvinestown, is of uncertain date. Its discovery 12 feet below the surface suggests that it was deliberately buried perhaps on account of its pagan origin, although there could be other reasons for it being hidden. Some years ago in Co. Cavan a stone figure was buried in the bog after several accidents occurred on the farm where it was kept.[28] The Enniskillen head has an unusually long neck, a feature which could be ithyphallic in origin. It occurs in another stone head, usually accepted as a pagan idol which came from an old church at Kilmanahin, Co. Kilkenny.[29] Long columnar necks were certainly shown on 'Celtic' figure-carvings in Britain and on the Continent, but in our present state of knowledge the two Irish examples with this feature can only be dated very tentatively to the pre-Christian period.

Wooden Idols

Wooden idols were also made by the Celts and displayed in woodland sanctuaries. A 'Celtic' sanctuary near Massalia (Marseilles), destroyed by Caesar, is described thus by Lucan:- 'And there were many dark springs running there, and grim-faced figures of gods uncouthly hewn by the axe from the untrimmed tree-trunk, rotted to whiteness.'[30] One such figure made of bog oak was found near Shercock in Co. Cavan in a bog at Ralaghan. It has a circular hole which was probably intended for a detachable phallus. This suggests that the idol was connected with fertility rites. Since it was found at the foot of Taghart mountain, which is remembered as the site of an ancient Lunasa harvest festival, it may have come from a sanctuary on top of the mountain. In post-medieval times (17th or 18th century) a survival of this festival consisted of a week-long festive assembly while in the present century young people visited Taghart every year on the first Sunday of August, a day known as Bilberry Sunday.[31]

A Non-Classical Art

It will be obvious from this account of 'Celtic' art, with its two-faced and three-faced gods, and its head idols shown without bodies or combined with beast heads, that 'Celtic' figure sculpture differs essentially from Classical sculpture. The Classical gods were depicted as idealized men and women. 'Celtic' artists, on the other hand, used the human figure in a non-realistic fashion, their aim being to express the spiritual potency and mysticism of their gods symbolically. This approach brings them far closer to Scythian and Near Eastern art than to the art of Greece and Rome.

1 **Head Idol, Corravilla, Co Cavan**
National Museum, Dublin (1966 : 112)
Height 18.4cm; Max Width 16.4cm; Max Thickness (at nose) 15.6cm

Only the facial area of this stone head has been dressed which could suggest that it was originally displayed in a niche, perhaps like the skull-niches of Entremont and Roquepertuse. The base seems to have been deliberately carved to allow the head to tilt to one side. The stone is a local type of dolerite or gabbro. In the 19th century the head was displayed with the three-faced Corleck head and the Corraghy janiform carving at Drumeague, beside Corleck. There is no evidence to show that it was originally associated with these carvings. About 1865 it was brought from Drumeague to Corravilla which is only about a mile from it.

The dignified remote expression is achieved mainly by the treatment of the large lentoid eyes. These have pronounced upper and lower lids enclosing a hollowed centre. The nose is spatulate with faint indications of nostrils. The mouth is a deep, straight groove with the lower lip accentuated by grooving the below it. The ears are indicated as convex ridges in low relief.

J Roy Soc Ant Ireland, 99, 1969, 104
Rynne, E, *C B A Research Report*, 9, 1972, 85, Pl VIII, 4.

2 **Head Idol, near Cavan town**
National Museum, Dublin (1967 : 185)
Height 13.1cm; Max Width 13cm; Max Thickness 16.3cm

Because only the facial area of the stone has been dressed it is possible that it, like the Corravilla head, was originally displayed in a niche. It is made of a calcareous, medium grained grit which could have come from the basal Carboniferous sandstones of the north Meath/Cavan area. It was found in a deserted house.

The face has a serene expression and the bulbous broad-oval eyes may be intended to represent closed eyes. No eyebrows or ears are indicated. The nose is spatulate and the mouth is a wide slit with upper and lower lips indicated.

J Roy Soc Ant Ireland, 100, 1970, 154-155.
Rynne, E, *C B A Research Report*, 9, 1972, 90 Pl XI, 4.

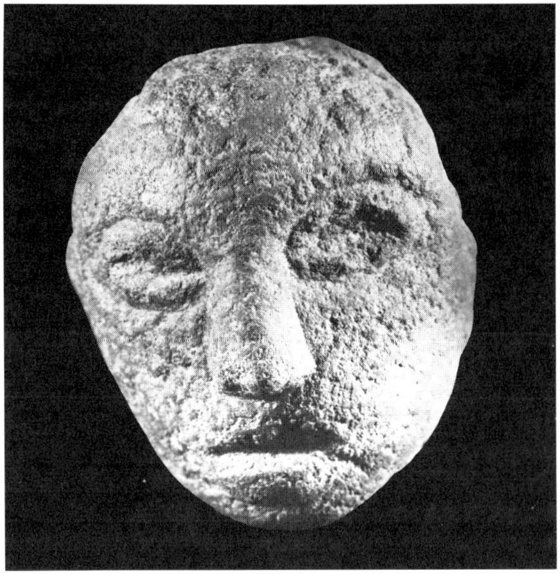
1

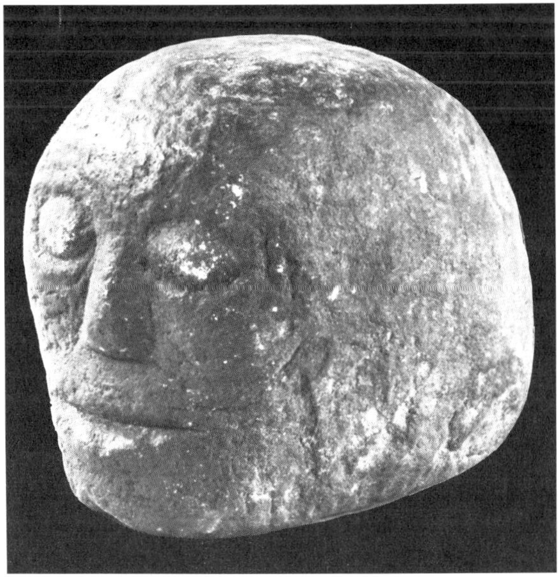
2

3 **Double Figure Dreenan townland, Boa Island, Co Fermanagh**
Caldragh Graveyard
Max Height 72.5cm; Max Width 46cm; Max Thickness 30.5cm

Janiform idol consisting of two busts set back to back, each with a large head and crossed limbs. Near the base are two parallel incised lines, generally interpreted as a wide belt, running horizontally on all four sides of the stone. The two faces are almost identical with large staring eyes outlined by ridges springing from the bridge of each spatulate nose. On both faces an upward-curling moustache is indicated, while each sharply pointed chin probably represents a beard. Pointed oval holes suggest open mouths, with perhaps the tip of the tongue appearing in one. On the same side as this is another unusual feature. One of the terminals of the crossed limbs, usually taken to be arms, looks very like a foot. This suggests that the limbs on this side represent legs in the so-called squatting Buddhic posture. On the opposite side the position of the crossed limbs above the phallus suggests that they are arms. The phallus is shown in low relief. On one of the narrow sides of the stone is a linear pattern, probably representing hair, set in the space between the two faces. It consists of an arrangement of narrow parallel bands roughly at right angles with one another. Although one strand crosses over another, the pattern cannot be accepted as true interlacing.

Between the two heads on top of the stone is a hollow (length 21.6cm; width 8.8cm; depth 12.7cm) which is better interpreted as a socket for holding an additional part of the idol than as a container for libations. This idol was in the Caldragh graveyard in 1841 when pencil sketches of it were made by Du Noyer. On the back of one of these Du Noyer recorded that a local informant remembered seeing a piece of stone set in the top hollow, which he took to be a small cross.

Lowry-Corry, Lady D, *P R I A*, 41, C, 1933, 200-4.
Rynne, E, *C B A Research Report*, 9, 1972, 85-6, Pl IX, 3.

4 **Three-faced Head, Corleck or Drumeague, Co Cavan**
National Museum, Dublin
Height 32cms

Known as the 'Corleck' head, this three-faced idol was found c. 1855 by a farmer in search of building stones either in Corleck or more probably in the neighbouring townland of Drumeague. A janiform carving of a human and ram's head may have been found with it (cf Corraghy Head).

It is carved from a block of siliceous sandstone, which could have come from Carrickaleck quarry, south east of Kingscourt. The three faces are similar but not identical. The mouth is shown as a narrow groove, the nose is spatulate and the round eyes are closely set. Supraorbital ridges are shown on only one face which also has a small hole cut in the centre of the mouth. Other 'Celtic' idols in Britain and on the Continent have this strange hole in the mouth and it is almost certainly an original feature of the Cavan idol. A small hole in the base of the head was probably a mortice for attaching the head to a pedestal or pillar.

Rynne, E, *C B A Research Report* 9, 1972, 83-84, Pl VIII, 3.
Barron, T J, *Clogher Record*, 1976, 98-102.
Raftery, J, *Catalogue for Rosc '67 Exhibition*, 132-3.

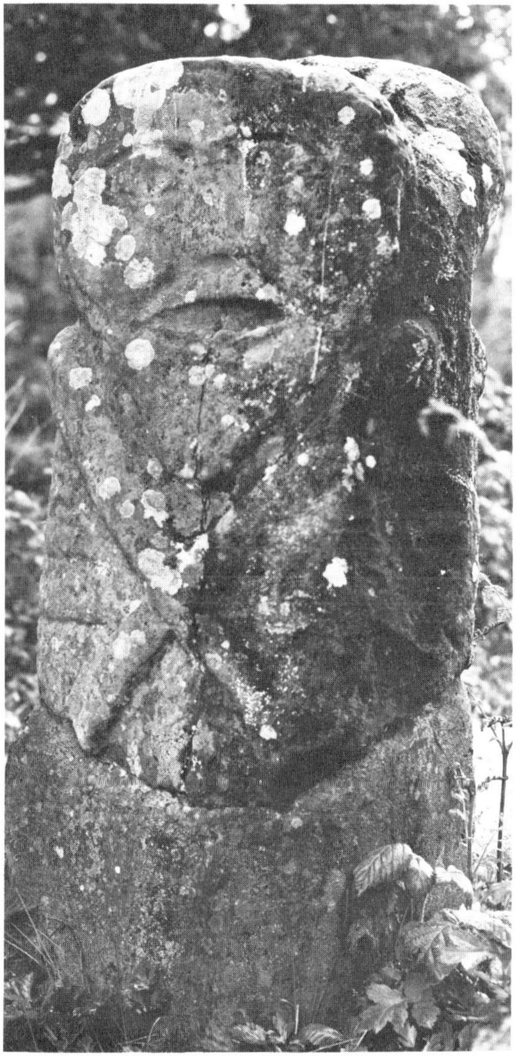

3

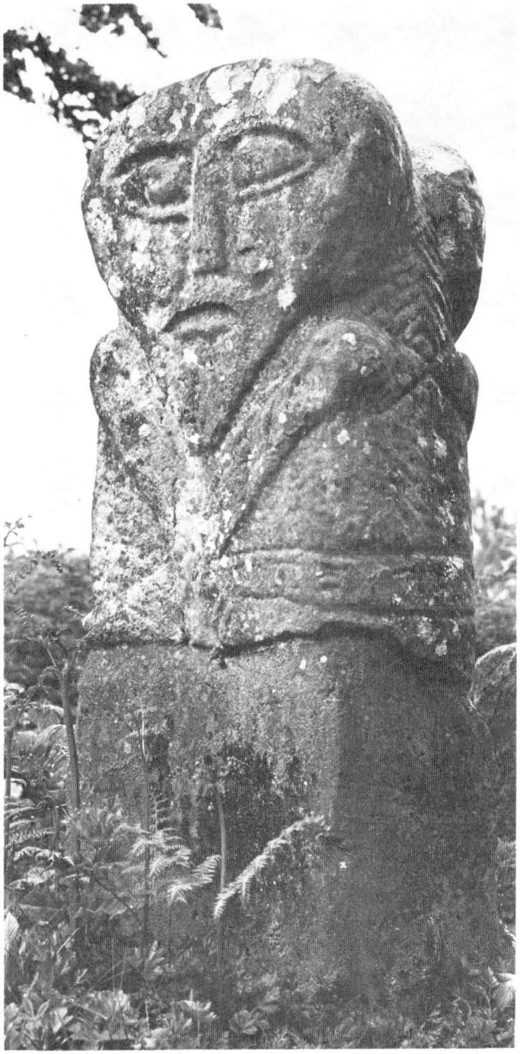

3

5 **Head from Janiform Carving, Corraghy, Co Cavan**
Lent to National Museum, Dublin by Thomas Barron, Bailieboro'
Height 44.5cm; Width 20.5cm; Thickness 26cm

This was found c. 1855, probably with the three-faced Corleck head, by a farmer in search of building material in the Corleck/Drumeague area of Co Cavan. According to local information collected by Thomas Barron the stones were gathered from an ancient site in the area to the north of the surviving Wedge grave in Drumeague townland. The site, now completely destroyed, was described as 'a monastery' 'an old castle' and as 'a pagan burial ground'.

Mr Barron, with the help of local informants, has identified this head as the surviving part of a janiform carving, the missing head being that of a ram. The ram part was destroyed about 1865 in an attempt to divide the stone. The head part was then set into the gable of a barn where it remained for more than a hundred years until it was acquired by Mr Barron. When it was removed from the barn in 1969 Mr Barron observed that the chiseling marks which remained after the ram portion of the stone had been severed were much fresher than the dressing of the rest of the stone. Moreover these marks had erased some of the original 'hair' from the back of the head.

The face is unusual in having a benign expression indicated by the upward curve of the mouth. Another unusual feature of the carving is the long neck with its thick flat rectangular base. The spatulate nose joins with the low supra-orbital ridges. Cheeks are notably flat while the narrow lentoid eyes have a scored line above them suggesting eye-lids. Hair is indicated by incised parallel lines; beard and side whiskers are shown in low relief. Ear cavities are present surrounded by a narrow pennanular ridge. The crown of the head is flat and smooth.

The reconstruction of this janiform carving is based on a drawing by the artist Bill Richards from Cavan.

Rynne, E, *C B A Research Report,* 9, 1972, 80, 85, Pl XI, 1.
Barron, T J, *Clogher Record,* 1976, 98-102.

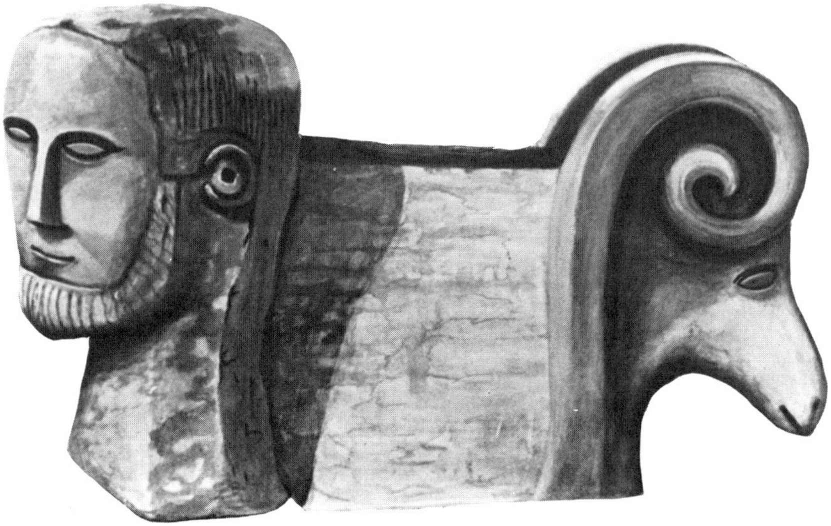

5

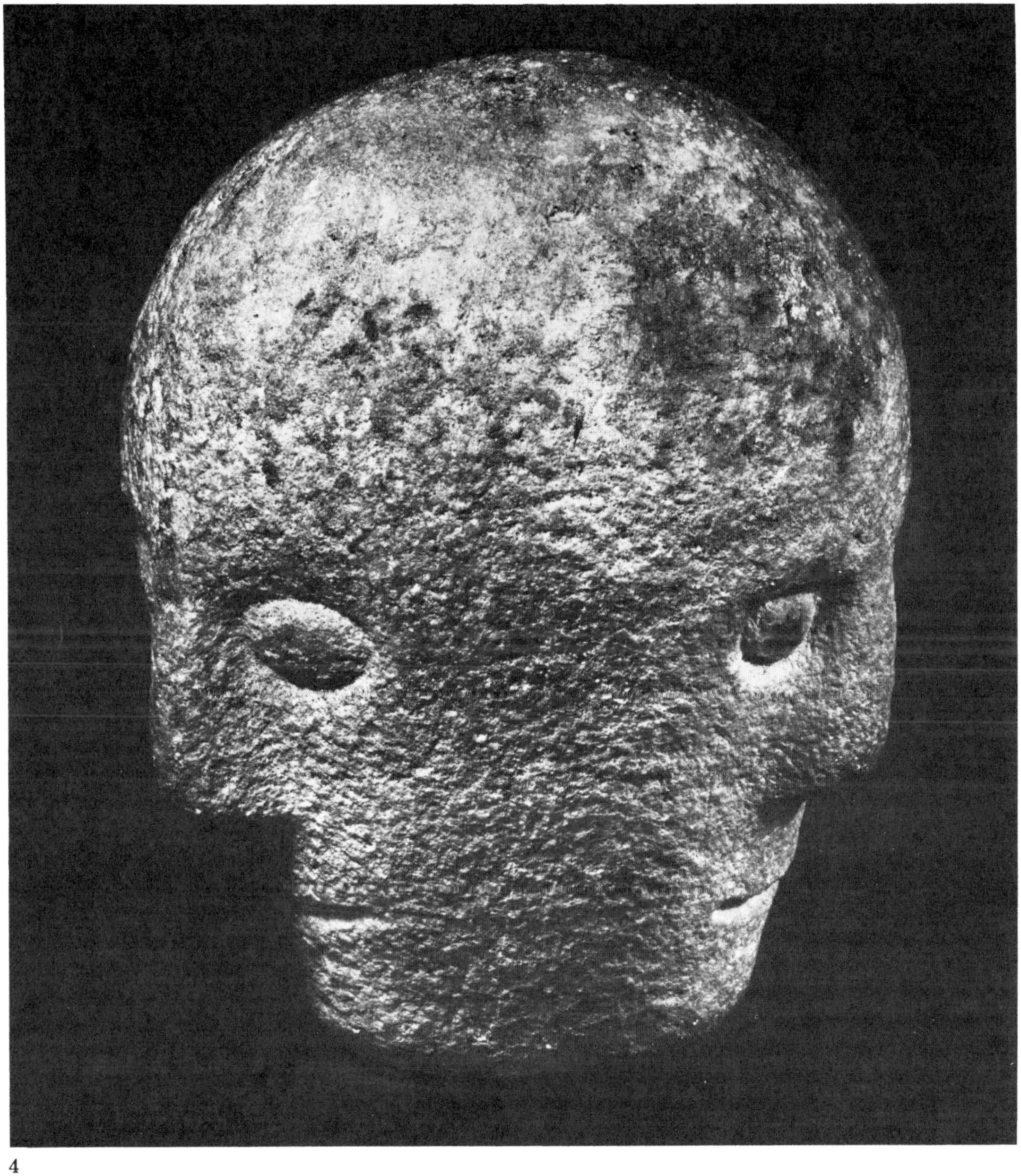

4

6 **Head Idol from Tonystick townland, Enniskillen**
On display at Mahon's Hotel, Irvinestown, Co Fermanagh
Height 49.5cm; Max Width 15cm

Discovered in the late 1960's when foundations were being dug for Agnew's garage (behind Fort Lodge) in Enniskillen. It was found at a depth of about 12 feet below the surface, near a site marked on the 1857 Ordnance Survey map as a 'chapel well'.

Made of hard sandstone it is distinguished by its long narrow face and disproportionately long neck. The eyes are no more than deep round holes and the wide slit mouth held three teeth, recently destroyed, which may have been made of bone or horn. The nose is straight sided with rounded ridge and without nostrils. The ill-defined chin tapers gradually to the long pole-like neck (23cms in length).

This is a roughly finished idol, its coarse pocked tooling marks being particularly noticeable on the neck. It is now set into the wall of the hotel lounge and the back of it cannot be examined. Its date is uncertain although it may be pre-Christian.

7 **Carved Deity from Lustymore Island, Co Fermanagh**
Now at Caldragh Graveyard, Boa Island
Height 70.7cm; Width 40cm; Thickness 17.8cm

Brought to Boa Island from the disused graveyard on nearby Lustymore Island. The figure has often been compared with the two-faced Boa Island idol. It is made of the same stone but unlike it is only carved on one face. It has the same kind of oversized head, although not so boldly carved. The top of the stone is cut to the circular shape of the head and the arms are also modelled. The left eye has not been fully carved, perhaps for some deliberate reason now obscure or because the carving of the deity was never completed. Lowry-Corry suggests that this may have been intended to represent a closed or blind eye.

The mouth is pointed oval with lips enclosing an oval shape. This suggests an open mouth but it is not recessed as on the Boa Island figure. The nose is a simple wedge shape. The arms and hands may be clearly seen and may rest on knees arranged in a squatting posture. There is not, however, any clear delineation of crossed legs.

Lowry-Corry, Lady D, *P R I A* 41C, 1933, 203-204, P1 VIII, Fig 2.
Rynne, E, *C B A Research Report,* 9, 1972, 86, P1 IX, 3.

8 **Wooden Idol, Ralaghan, near Shercock, Co Cavan**
National Museum, Dublin
Height 114cm

A large figure of bog-oak found in a bog. It represents a standing figure, without arms and with a severe facial expression. The upper part of the body is roughly shaped and formless. The lower part contains a neatly drilled circular hole usually interpreted as a socket for a phallus. Megaw, however has suggested that it could represent the female vulva. The shapely legs are set on a small peg of wood which may have served as a tenon to fix the idol in a standing position. The figure is often compared with another armless wooden figure from Dagenham in Essex which also has a similarly placed circular hole.

Megaw, J V S, *Art of the European Iron Age,* 1970, 164, Pl 280.
Ross, A, *Pagan Celtic Britain,* 1967, 35, Fig 5.
Piggott, S, *The Druids,* 1968, 85, Fig 31.

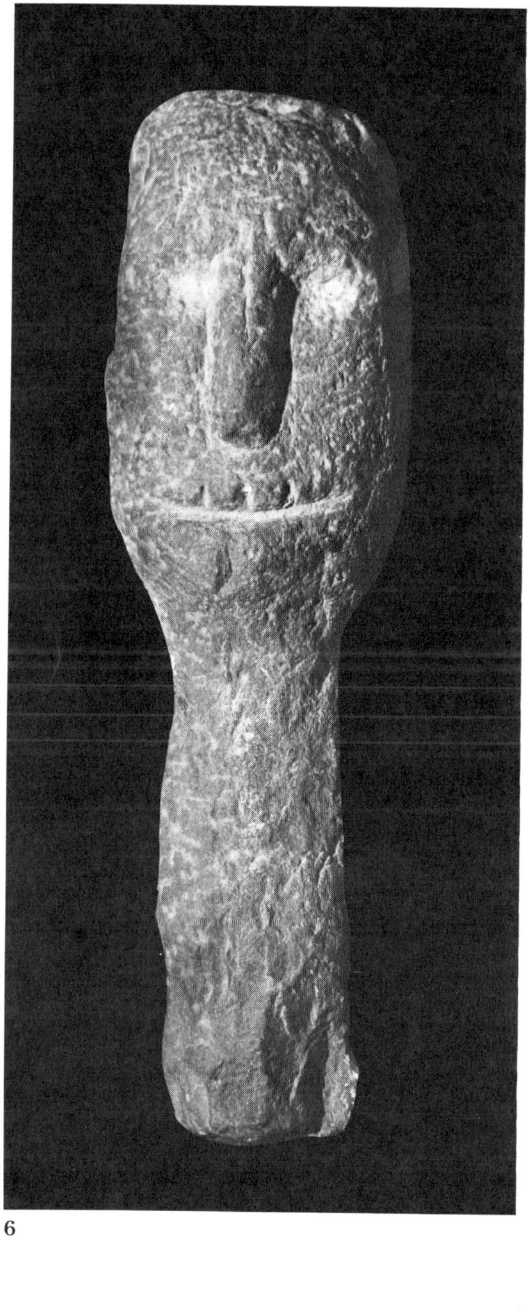

6

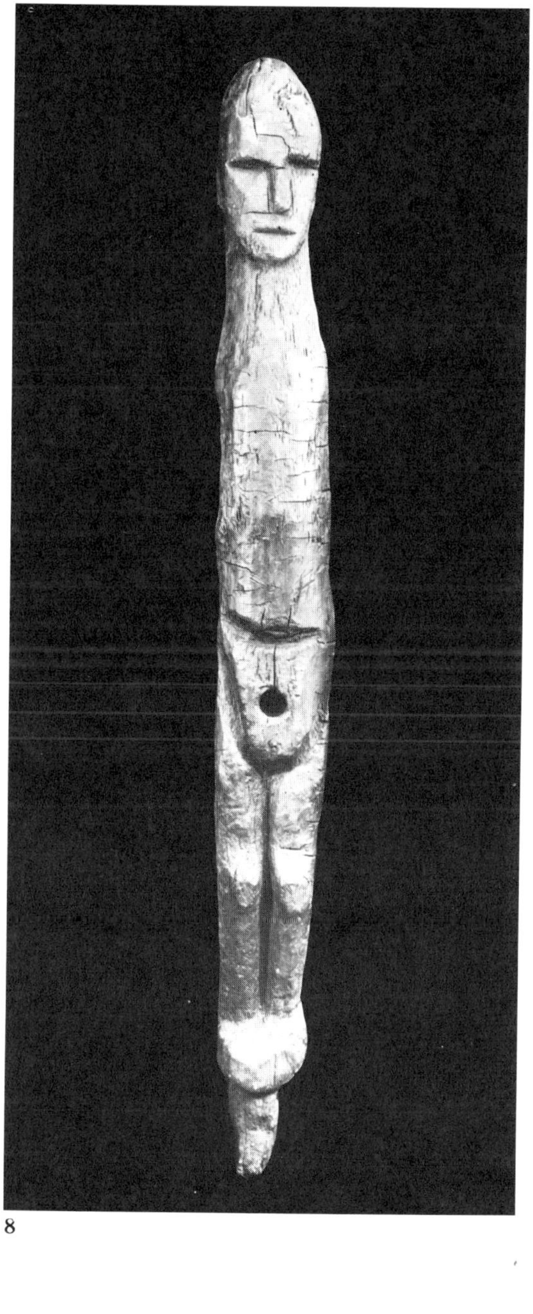

8

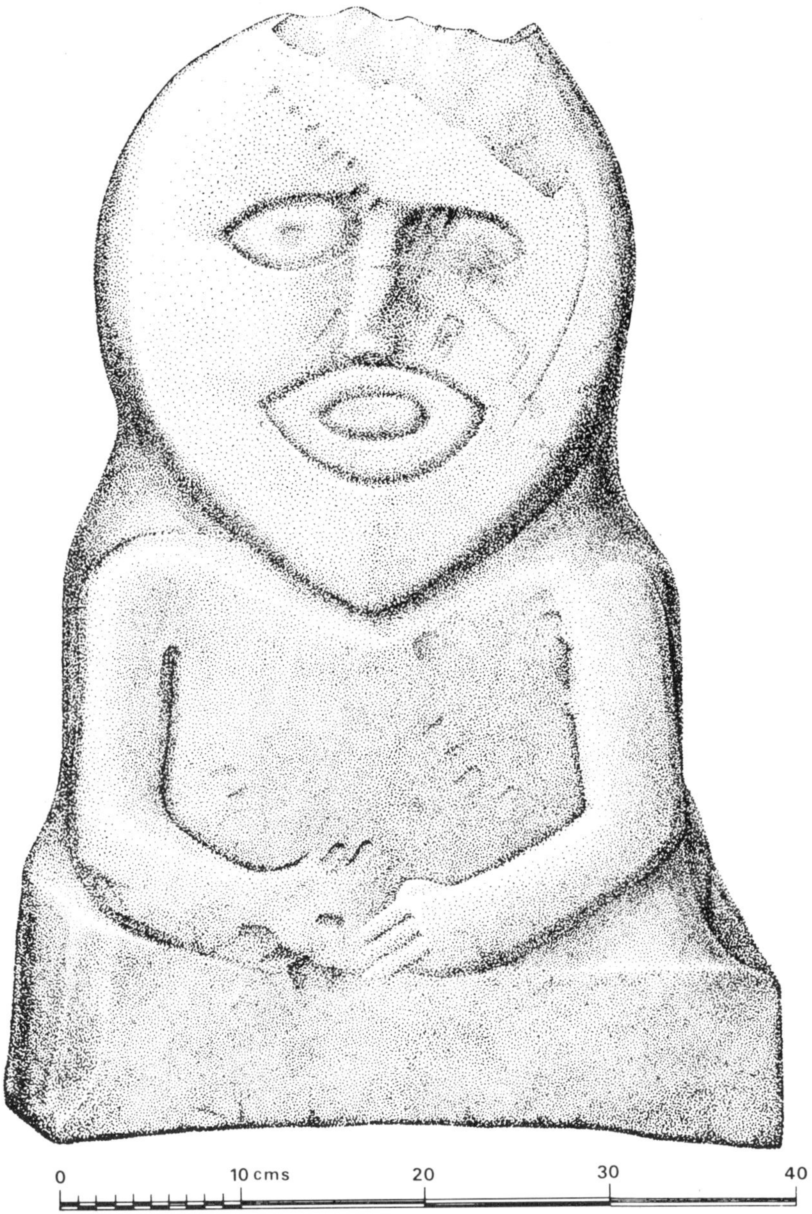

7

Christianity

Statues and High Crosses: 9th to 11th century

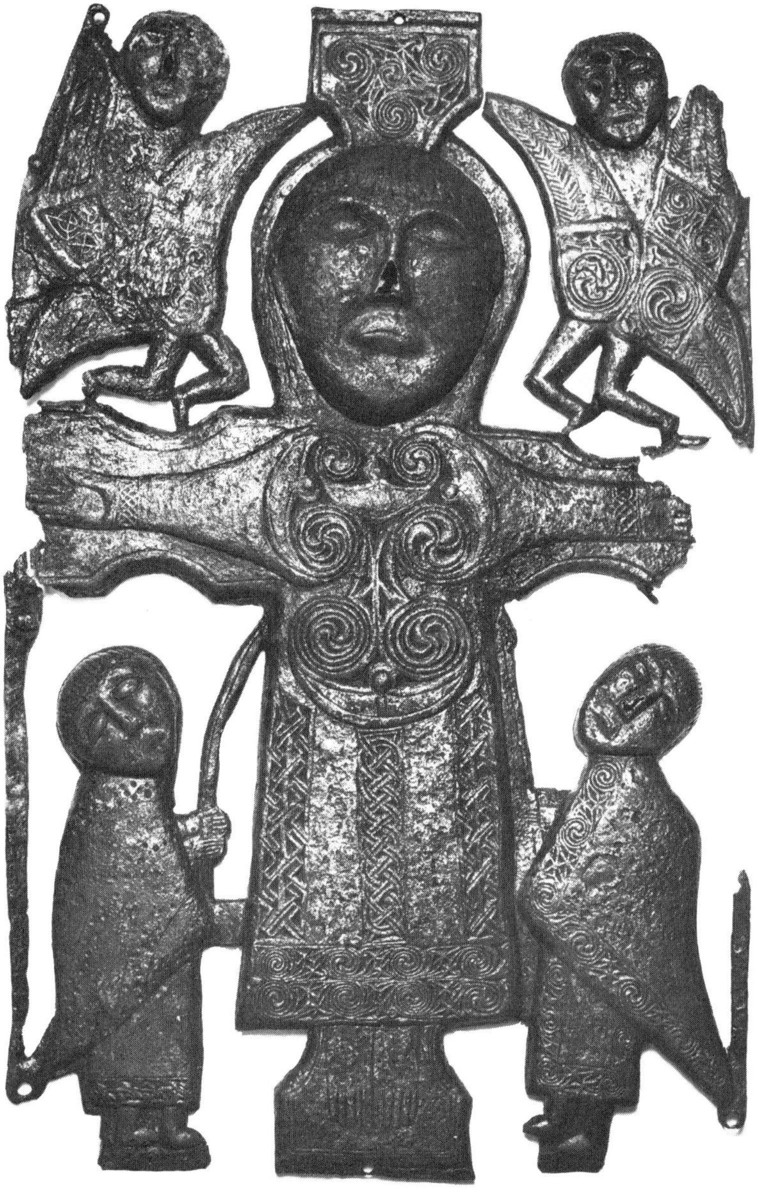

Crucifixion plaque from Athlone

Following on the introduction of Christianity to the Irish, the Church there was organized on diocesan lines with a bishop assigned to each diocese. The same system operated successfully in Britain but in Ireland it met with only relative success. This was largely due to the absence there of the kind of urban centres and administration which existed in Britain. During the 6th and 7th centuries monasteries, which had begun as hermitages chosen for their remoteness and isolation, replaced the earlier Irish churches as focal points of Christianity. Some of the earlier establishments, such as Armagh and Clonard, actually became monasteries.

The earliest stone monuments of the Christian Church, perhaps as early as the 5th century, are pillars engraved with a simple cross. By the 6th century these cross-inscribed pillars sometimes contain Irish inscriptions in Ogham writing. The free-standing High Crosses, an invention of the 8th century, were followed in the 9th and 10th century by elaborately carved Scripture High Crosses. Statues as such, like those on White Island in Fermanagh, are quite unusual.

Gradual Change from Paganism to Christianity

The advent of Christianity is unlikely to have brought about abrupt changes in such isolated areas as Fermanagh and Cavan. Apart from a rather doubtful visit by Patrick to the Mag Slécht area of West Cavan,[1] and a possible foundation by St Senach at Derrybrusk the early missionaries do not appear to have penetrated into this part of Ireland, so that Christian beliefs must have percolated slowly into the region. Christian missionaries tended to be tolerant of pagan practices and where possible modified and transmuted rather than destroyed cherished beliefs. The ancient oral learning was written down without excessive censorship, the poetic traditions were allowed to flourish. This kind of tolerance could explain why four pagan idols from Fermanagh were found in a Christian context. In one case — that of the Double Figure from the old graveyard on Boa Island — the pagan idol may even have been used to support a cross.

Christian Figure-Carving in the 7th and 8th centuries

Although several centuries may have elapsed between the carving of the latest pagan idols and the earliest Christian figures in the late 7th and 8th century, there is an apparent continuity in terms of style and in attitude to representation. The naturalism of Classical art is once again eschewed and the Christian stone-carvers continue as in the earlier tradition to express mystical attributes and spiritual power symbolically in highly formalized and mysteriously potent images. In manuscripts and metalwork the same approach is apparent. There is no attempt at naturalistic representation and the figure is once again disproportionately dominated by the head, formerly such a powerful symbol for the pagan cults. In stonework this lack of realism is further emphasized by the flatness of the figure-carving, merely an incised outline in some cases. This continued to be the typical stone-carving style until almost fully-rounded sculptural figures appeared on Scripture Crosses, largely due to the stimulus of Carolingian ivories.

The White Island Statues

The most remarkable Irish examples of Early Christian figure carving are six statues from Fermanagh, on White Island in Lower Lough Erne, carvings of such exceptional quality that they must be regarded as products of a master craftsman. They were found at different times, some built into the walls of a 12th century church. The discovery of an unfinished statue suggests that the carving was actually done on the site. The six completed statues, all of quartzite, have sockets on top. They were apparently designed as three pairs of caryatids (figures used as supporting pillars), each pair a different height.

Carved in the 9th, 10th or 11th century

The statues are clearly contemporaneous and can be reliably dated by comparative methods to sometime within the period of the 9th to the 11th century. Their three-dimensional sculptural form and certain details of their iconography provide strong links with the Scripture High Crosses, which are dated independently to the same time. Comparisons can also be made with illustrated psalters of this period, which were probably used as models by the Master of White Island. Even stronger dating evidence is available if one accepts the widely held view that medieval artists (when depicting earlier personages and events) were never archaistic but portrayed their subjects in contemporary costume, and with contemporary accoutrements. One of the statues holds a crooked crozier, probably an enshrined crozier, of 9th, 10th or 11th century type. Another wears a penannular brooch with circular terminals, possibly representing a Viking thistle-brooch or else a somewhat earlier type like the Kilmainhan brooch. The thistle brooches, so called on account of their bristling knob terminals were in common use by the native population as well as by Vikings from as far afield as Scotland and Norway during the late 9th and 10th centuries.

Earlier Dating Unacceptable

These statues have fired the imaginations of many antiquaries whose learned papers one can largely dismiss as fanciful. One theory is that they illustrate an episode in the life of St Patrick, recorded in the *Vita Tripartita.*[2] A more common view is that they represent pagan gods. This latter interpretation is of interest in being an acknowledgement of the stylistically archaic quality of these statues, particularly in the treatment of the face. The superficial resemblance between these statues and Celtic idols may be totally accidental, but it could be due to the lingering of early traditions in this part of Fermanagh, for example the tradition of regarding the human head as the pre-eminent symbol of divinity.

Contemporary Costume

The garment worn by five of the six statues is the full-length 'léine' or linen tunic so often depicted on High Crosses as well as on two locally made metal shrines — the Breac Maodhóg and the Soiscél Molaise. It is not of much use as dating evidence because it was a garment, derived from Mediterranean styles, which was worn over a very long period in Ireland by men, women and children of the upper classes. It sometimes had an embroidered hem, probably indicated by the raised border on the statues. An unusual feature of the White Island examples is the central seam down the front of the garment.

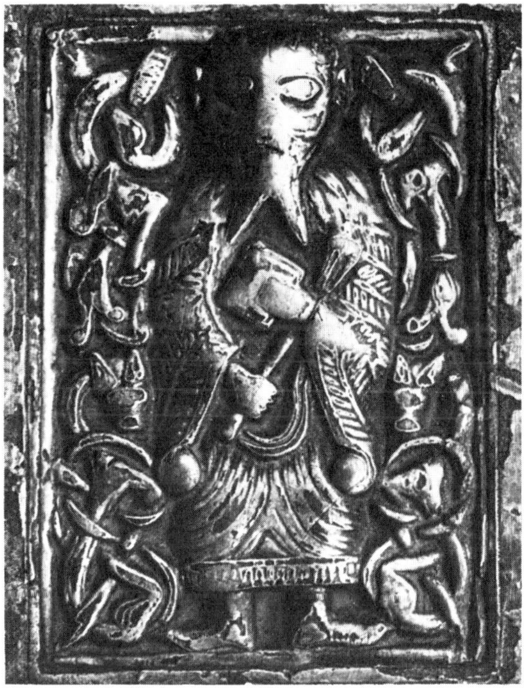

Detail from Soiscél Molaise

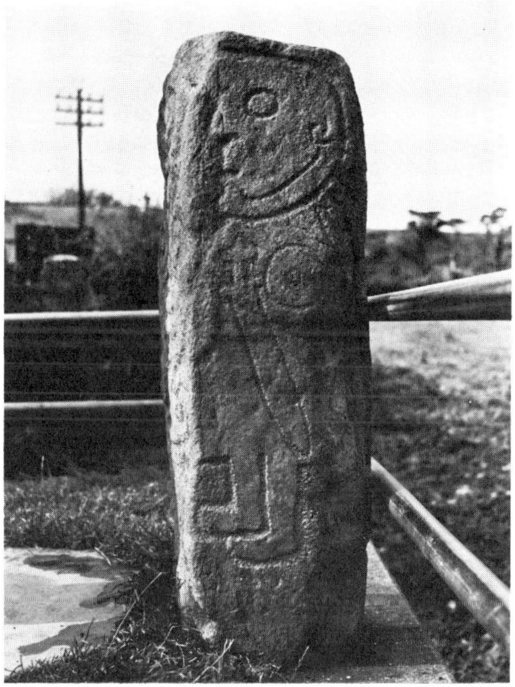

Warrior on Carndonagh Pillar, Co Donegal

The Identity of the Statues

The Christian symbolism of five of the six statues is easy to detect. Three of the statues probably represent different aspects of Christ and are good illustrations of the Early Christian approach to iconography. Another statue may be Christ or St Anthony and the fifth is likely to be King David. The sixth, the smallest caryatid, is such a strange companion for the others, a grinning lewd woman in the midst of solemn-eyed ecclesiastics, that one can understand why earlier writers proposed a pagan origin for the group. However it too can be demonstrated as fitting into the overall Christian framework.

Early Christian Approach to Iconography

Three of the statues have been identified as representations of Christ, and following Early Christian patterns of iconography, were intended not as portraits in the modern sense but to transmit theological ideas and convey spiritual meanings. So Christ holding a pair of griffins — symbols of the dual nature of God — illustrates one of the basic and complex mysteries of Christianity. The matching caryatid of Christ the warrior almost certainly alludes to the Second Coming of Christ in power and great glory. Christ holding a Gospel book is probably a direct reference to the Gospel as being the Word of God, as well as an allusion to the missionary role of the Church.

In the same way scenes from the Old Testament, illustrated on High Crosses, were considered as prefigurations of events from the New Testament. David's role was seen as foreshadowing Christ's role, and so on. If the congregations on White Island were accustomed to thinking along these lines it is quite possible that at least at a popular level they regarded these statues as reincarnations of Irish mythological and historical figures. Christ, for example, may have been seen as a reincarnation of Cú Chulainn. Indeed Sharkey[3] has suggested that 'the Christian missionaries exploited this appeal to the Celtic imagination in laying the foundations of the new religion.'

Function of Caryatids?

No one has yet produced a wholly satisfactory explanation of how these caryatids might have functioned. The best suggestion is probably Françoise Henry's[4] — that they supported the steps of an ambo (a pulpit or preaching chair in the early church). This would account for their varying height and their arrangement in pairs, with each pair perhaps supporting a wooden step. However the pairs vary slightly in height and this variation could be augmented depending on how much of the stone appeared below the actual carving. This could allow for a reconstruction with each caryatid supporting a step set into the wall of the church. Another possibility is that each pair of caryatids supported two beams, set apart, the ends of which were fixed in the wall. A wide wooden platform resting on each pair of beams would still produce a stepped arrangement.

Ambones

A few early ambones have survived or been reconstructed in Italy, notably in Ravenna Cathedral[5] and in St Mary's Church at Castel-Saint Elia near Nepi.[6] The many references to them in early documentary sources are also informative. The ambo at St Sophia's in Constantinople constructed by Justinian was ascended by two flights of stairs, one from the west and the other from the east, and was covered by a canopy resting on eight columns.[7] The annals of the Four Masters refer to the destruction of the 'old preaching chair' in Armagh during the fire of 1020 AD. We are not told whether the chair was made of wood or stone. In the same fire the stone church with its lead roof was destroyed. An ambo may well have been standard equipment in all early monasteries. In the early 9th century plan of an ideal Carolingian monastery, preserved in the library of St Gall, the ambo is shown in the monks' church along with two lecterns for the Epistle and Gospel.[8]

Liturgical Function of Ambones

The ambo was used, like a modern pulpit, as a platform from which sermons were preached. It was also used by different officiating clergy to proclaim the gospel, epistle, litanies, psalms and any other communications intended for the congregation. An interesting refinement, which may not however be as early as the 9th or 10th century, consisted of reading the gospel at a higher level than the epistle.

None of the recorded information provides details of how ambones were actually made. Nor is it possible on the basis of comparisons with surviving continental ambones to provide a convincing reconstruction of the proposed White Island ambo.

A reconsideration of the iconography of the White Island statuary in the light of their possible function as ambo caryatids is revealing. We have seen that the statues were not simply portraits but were intended to transmit Christian ideas. Two of the subjects, Christ holding the Gospel and David the Psalmist, could be regarded as particularly appropriate carvings for a preaching chair, referring in a most direct way to the use of the ambo for reading the Gospel and singing psalms.

Alternative Suggestions for the use of the caryatids

One of the statues — Christ with Gospel book — has two small sockets on top instead of one. The top of the matching statue — the grotesque female — now badly damaged, may also have had two sockets. This could mean that they had a different function from the other caryatids and were perhaps used as supports for an altar. A similar function is suggested for another statue found near Lismore Cathedral in Co Waterford, which may have had an inscription on it referring to 'the table of the Lord'.[9] This inscription would also be appropriate if the caryatids supported a credence-table (small side table for eucharistic elements before consecration). The other two pairs of caryatids might have been used as jambs for sedilia (stone seats for priests, set in church wall) or possibly to support a screen isolating the sanctuary from the rest of the church.

Earlier Church on White Island?

It has been assumed, probably correctly, that these caryatids belonged to a monastic church of 9th, 10th or 11th century date on White Island. There are historical references to monasteries of this period in this part of Lough Erne, one called Devenish Bavagh, another called Eo-Inis. But because the original Irish name of White Island has not been established, one cannot be sure that either of these is to be identified with White Island. Archaeological evidence for an earlier church is also inconclusive. A small portion of the present church was excavated in 1959.[10] Sleeper trenches for timber structures were uncovered but the excavated area was not extensive enough to indicate whether or not these represented earlier wooden churches on the site. This means that the statues themselves represent the strongest evidence for an earlier monastic foundation, situated on or near the site of the present 12th century church. Stone churches were being built at the time the statues were made but given the enduring popularity of wooden churches in Early Christian Ireland, the statues are just as likely to have been incorporated into a wooden church as into a stone one.[11]

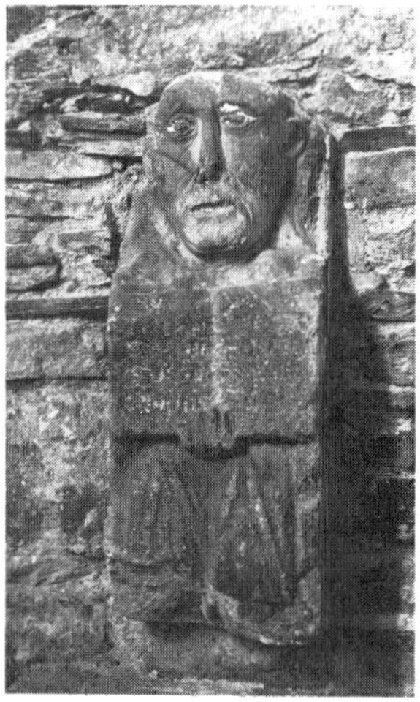

Statue from Lismore, Co Waterford

Other Irish Statues

Statues like the White Island ones are extremely rare. One was found near Lismore Cathedral, Co. Waterford. It is a caryatid, the same size as the smallest of the Fermanagh statues. It is of a male seated figure holding an open book which may have contained an inscription.[12] Another very simply carved statue was found at Downdaniel in Co. Cork which may have served as a caryatid.[13] It is about the same height as the largest of the White Island statues. The figure with a simple block-like body is carved on one side and a double cross is cut on the back.

Another carved stone from Killadeas, which is on the mainland about 3½ miles south west of White Island, may have served for a time as a caryatid. It resembles the White Island statues in many ways and may have been an attempt by an inferior stone-carver to copy one of the White Island caryatids.

High Crosses

When comparing iconographic details of the White Island statues with those of Scripture Crosses, the examples quoted are usually from outside the Lough Erne area. The reason for this is that although similar scripture crosses are to be found in Fermanagh, all of them are broken and so badly weathered that they have lost all their fine sculptural details. The earliest and most significant group of crosses comes from the monastery of Galloon, founded in the 6th century by the same St Tighernach who founded the monastery at Clones. It must have been a wealthy monastery for it boasts of the remains of at least three Scripture Crosses, which probably belong to the late 9th and early 10th century.[14] Another cross-shaft now at Lisnaskea is believed to have been brought there from Galloon. The only bit of figure carving at Inishkeen is a very weathered head with peculiar ass-like ears carved on a broken cross-shaft. The cross-shaft at Boho in Co. Fermanagh is very like the cross at Drumcliff in Co. Sligo and is probably not earlier than the 11th century.

Galloon

Two of the White Island statues have been tentatively identified as King David and St Anthony. In this connection it is noteworthy that the Galloon cross fragments, which are roughly contemporary with the White Island statues, indicate a marked interest in depicting scenes from the life of David. On the east cross two of the scenes have been identified as David with Jonathan, and the anointing of David. The anointing is also shown on the west cross as well as an illustration of David breaking the jaws of the lion. St Anthony appears on the east cross accompanied by St Paul.

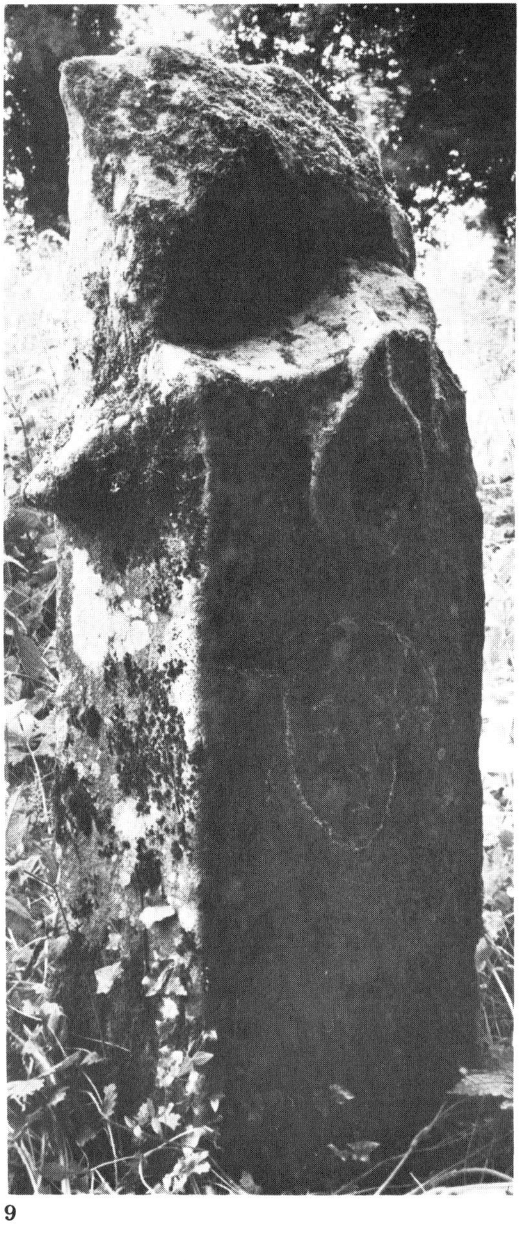
9

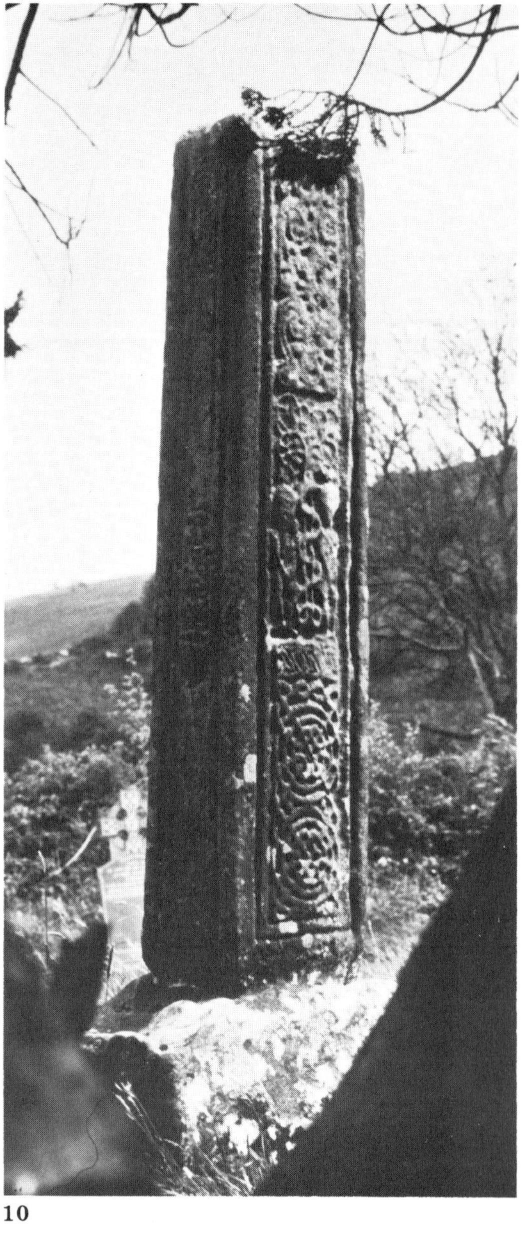
10

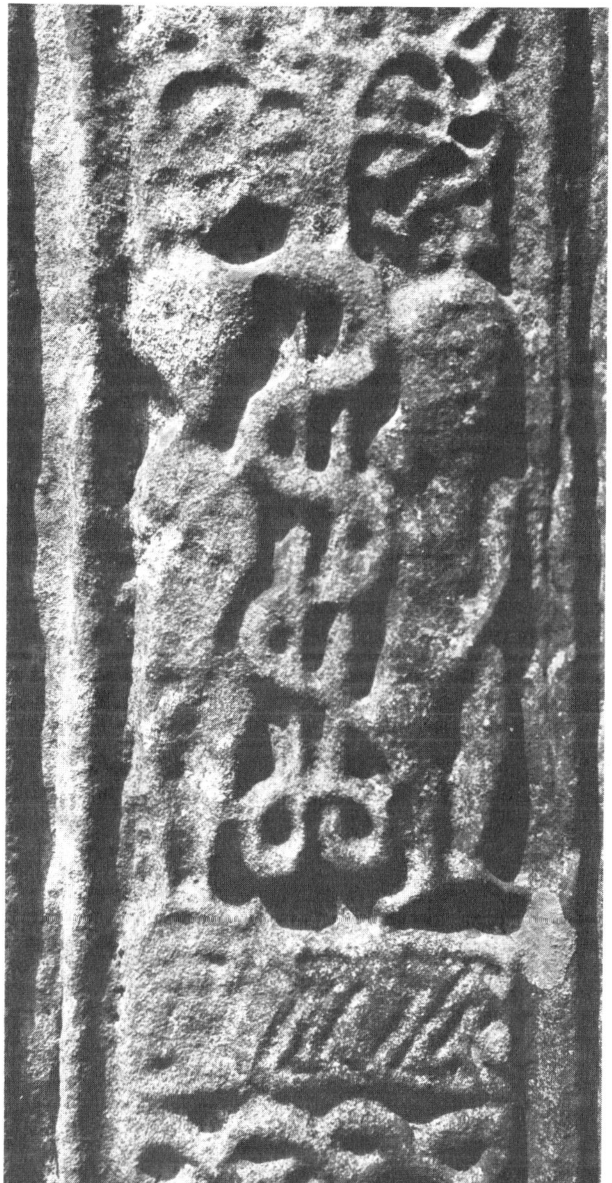

10

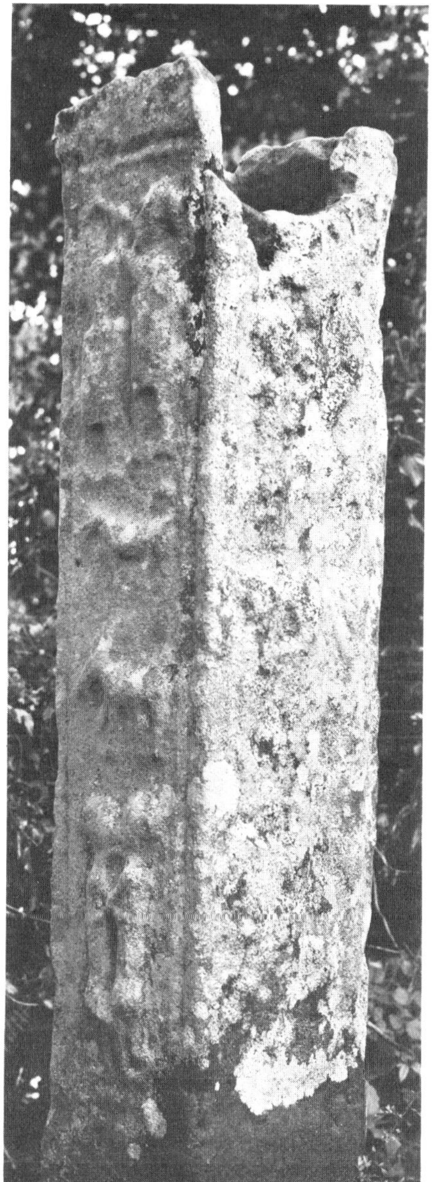

11

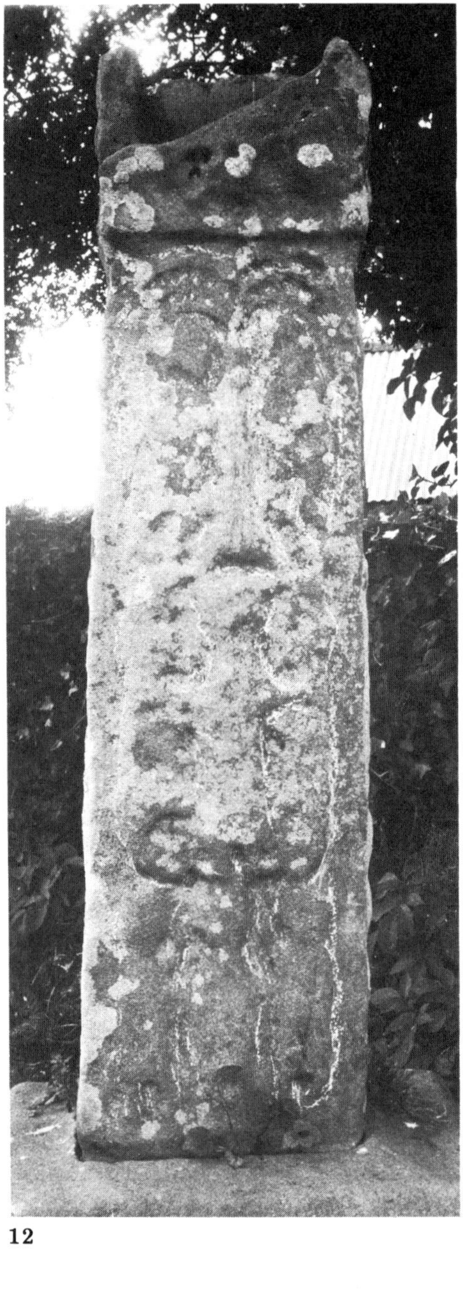
12

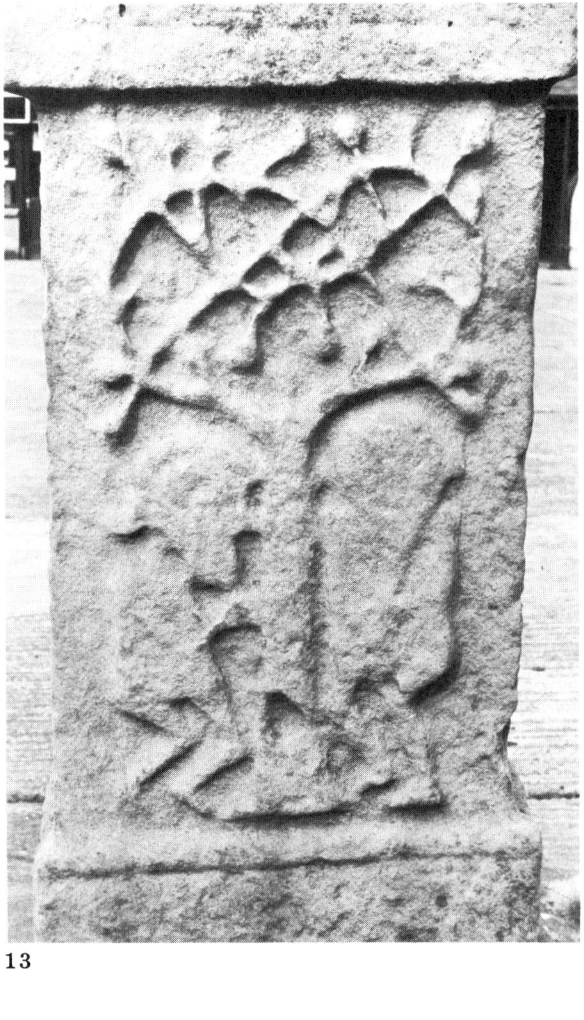
13

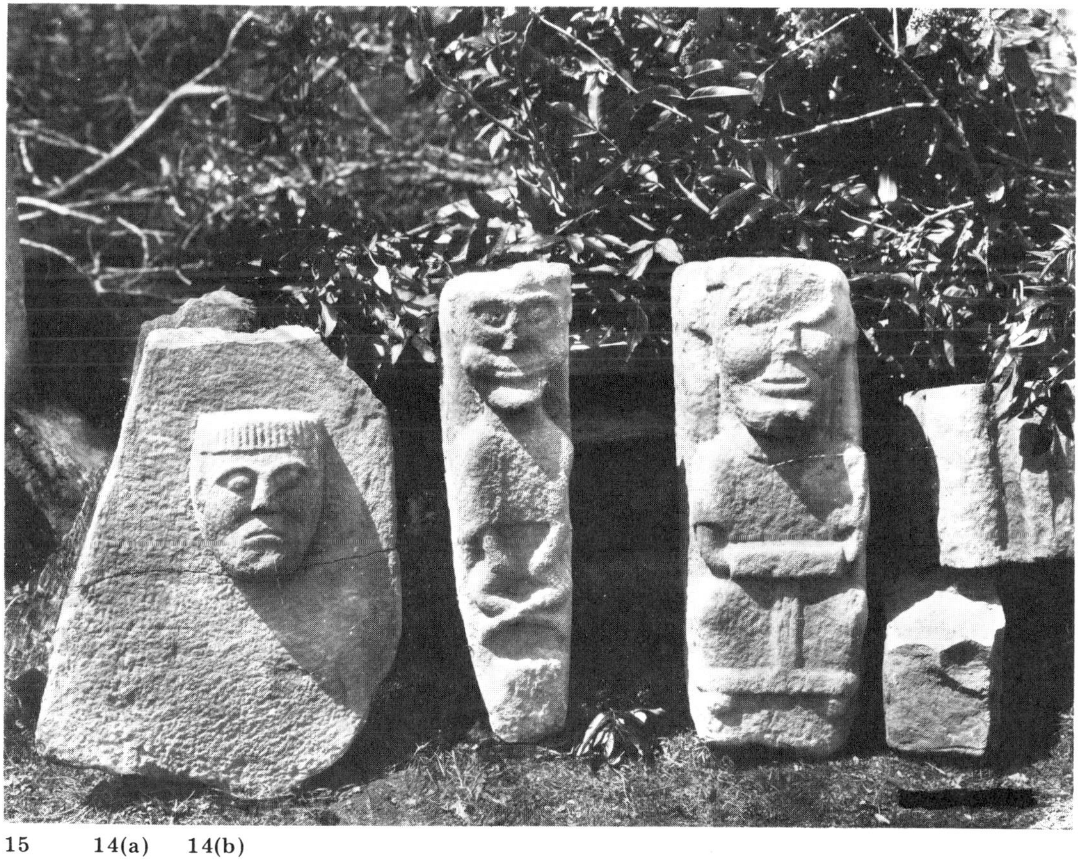

15 14(a) 14(b)

9 **Shaft of High Cross, Inishkeen Island, Fermanagh**

10 **Shaft of High Cross, Toneel graveyard, Boho, Fermanagh**

11 **Shaft of East Cross, Galloon Island, Fermanagh**

12 **Shaft of West Cross, Galloon Island, Fermanagh**

13 **Shaft of High Cross, Lisnaskea, Fermanagh**

14(a) **Six Statues from White Island, Lower Lough Erne, Co Fermanagh**
Grotesque Figure
Height of stone 60.5cm; Height of statue 47.5cm; Width 15cm; Thickness 19cm

Female figure with bulging cheeks and crossed legs, naked except for the round-necked cape covering the upper part of the body. Hands resting on both thighs are indicating the genital area. Damage to the top of the stone has destroyed much of the narrow head band and most of the socket. It is possible that this caryatid possessed two sockets like those on its 'partner'. The face is quite distorted, the eyes framed by a heavy ridge, the mouth between puffed-out cheeks fixed in a wide grin.

The identity of this statue remains elusive as does the precise nature of its symbolism. It certainly does not represent a chaste young girl at Ettlinger has suggested, but rather a lascivious beguiling woman displaying her power to lead men astray. It could be interpreted as an illustration of Lust and a warning to the monks against the sins of the flesh. The crossed legs, recalling the squatting Buddhic posture of pagan gods, suggest once again the survival of earlier traditions in this locality. One might even go so far as to suggest that the Master of White Island was deliberately echoing archaic forms in order to enhance the power of this image. A further clue to the meaning of this statue is to be found in Muiredach's Cross, a 10th century Scripture High Cross at Monasterboice in Co Louth. A somewhat similar female figure with splayed legs is shown in its magnificently composed Judgement scene, where she is significantly placed among the Damned. The relationship of these two female figures to grotesque carvings of women known as Sheila-na-gigs is uncertain and will be discussed in the following chapter.

Ettlinger, E, *Ogam.* 10, 1958, 271.
O'Driscoll, D, *J Roy Soc Antiq Ireland*, 1942, 116

14(b) **Christ holding Gospel book**
Height of stone 62cm; Height of statue 56.5cm; Width 22cm; Thickness 19cm.
Front Socket: 9cm square; Depth 5cm; Back Socket: Width 8.5cm; Depth 5cm.

Seated figure holding a rectangular object on his knees, probably a copy of the Gospels, perhaps within a box shrine. He wears a short-sleeved collared 'léine' with a front seam between the waist and the hem. The upper part of the head has been severely damaged since it was drawn by Du Noyer over a hundred years ago. The top of this statue differs from the others in having two small sockets, one open at the back like the larger sockets. Wakeman in 1880 commented on these:- 'one evidently a socket, while the other is simply a bevel for the drainage of wall water from the timber once inserted in the mortise.'

This statue probably represents Christ, although the Evangelists are sometimes portrayed in a similar manner in illuminated manuscripts. In the 'Book of Kells' Christ is represented thus, in a seated position and holding the Gospel.

Wakeman, *J R S A I*, 15, 1880, 292.

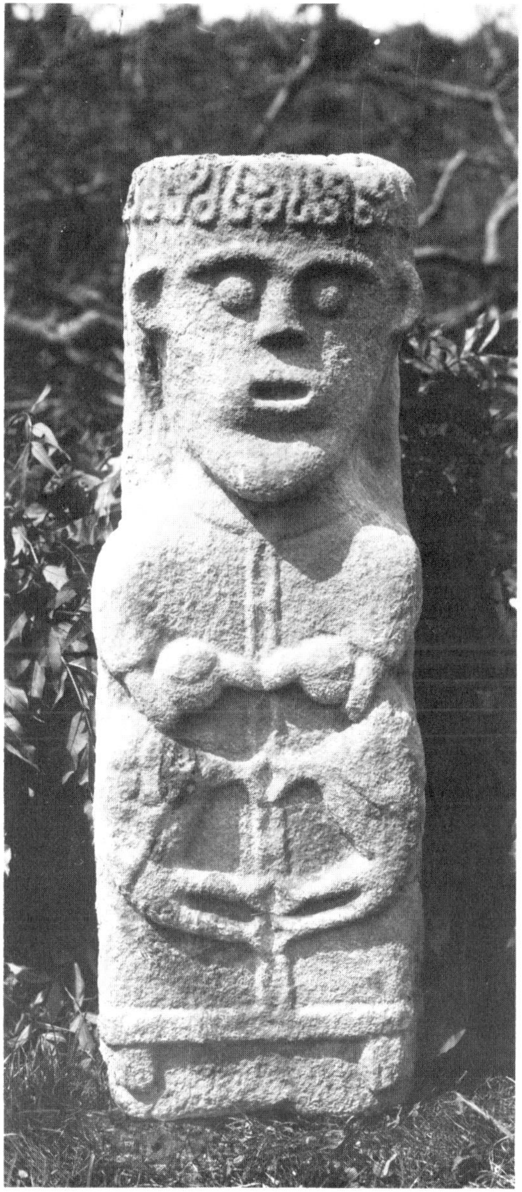

14(c)

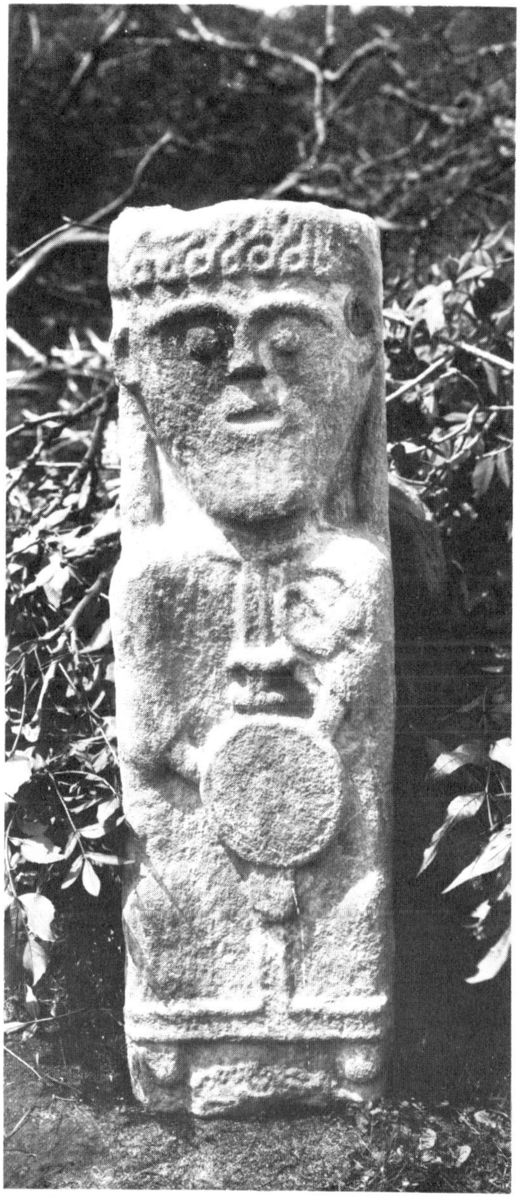

14(d)

14(c) Christ with Griffins

Height of stone 80.5cm; Height of statue 78cm; Width 28cm; Thickness 28.7cm.
Socket: Width 12.5cm; Length 16cm (to wall); Depth 1.7cm.

Closely resembles its 'partner' the statue of Christ in warrior attire. It has the same curly fringed hair-style, similar facial features and wears an identical tunic. The figure grasps with both hands the necks of a pair of affronted griffins — fabulous monsters with the head, wings and claws of an eagle and the body of a lion. These make it possible to identify this statue as Christ. Griffins symbolize the dual nature of Christ, divine represented by bird, human by animal. An illuminated page in the Turin Gospel Book contains two panels with a figure holding a similar pair of griffins.

One of the sides of this statue is covered with a broad-ribboned interlaced pattern, which possibly represents the side of a high-backed throne.

Hall, J, *Dictionary of Subjects and Symbols in Art,* 1974, 143.
Henry, F, *Irish Art during the Viking Invasions 800-1020 AD,* 1967, 193, Pl 39.

14(d) Christ in Warrior Attire

Height of stone 79.5cm; Height of statue 75.5cm; Width 25cm; Thickness 28cm.
Socket: Width 13.5cm; Length 18.5cm (to wall); Depth 1.7cm.

This second statue with fringed hair style is armed with a short sword and a small round shield, wears a brooch below the left shoulder and is in a seated position. The brooch, distinguished by its round terminals, may be a Viking 'thistle' brooch, a late 9th or 10th century type of penannular brooch. Alternatively it could represent an earlier kind of brooch, of 8th or 9th century date, like the one found at Kilmainhan, Dublin. Neither the sword nor the shield are closely datable.

This statue is identified as Christ in his role as King of Glory on his Second Coming on earth in power and triumph. Helen Roe believes that the concept of an armed Christ derives from some psalter illustration, possibly one to accompany psalm XXIII, the final verses of which were considered to foretell the Second Coming. The Utrecht Psalter dated to c. 820 AD, contains an illustration of an armed Christ as does a later copy of the same text, the Canterbury Psalter (BM Harley 603).

The warrior Christ is also depicted on two Scripture Crosses of roughly the same date as the White Island statues. On the tall cross at Monasterboice, Co Louth, he wears the long tunic similar to that on the White Island statue and carries the same kind of shield with a rim around its edge. On the Market Cross in Kells, Co Meath he is clad in knee-length trousers. On both crosses Christ is appropriately accompanied by similarly armed hosts. The warrior depicted on the Carndonagh pillar may also be Christ although he is more usually interpreted as David. Since David was seen as a prefiguration of Christ it is possible that the armed figure was intended to represent simultaneously both Christ and David.

Roe, H M, *The High Cross of Kells,* 1966, 28-30
Henry, F, *Irish Art during the Viking Invasions 800-1020 AD,* 1967, P1 III.

14(e) David

Height of stone 105cm; Height of statue 85.5cm; Width 30.3cm; Thickness 24cm.
Socket: Width 12.5cm; Length 15cm (to wall); Depth 2.1cm.

This figure is identified as David by his gesture towards the mouth — a reference to David's role as

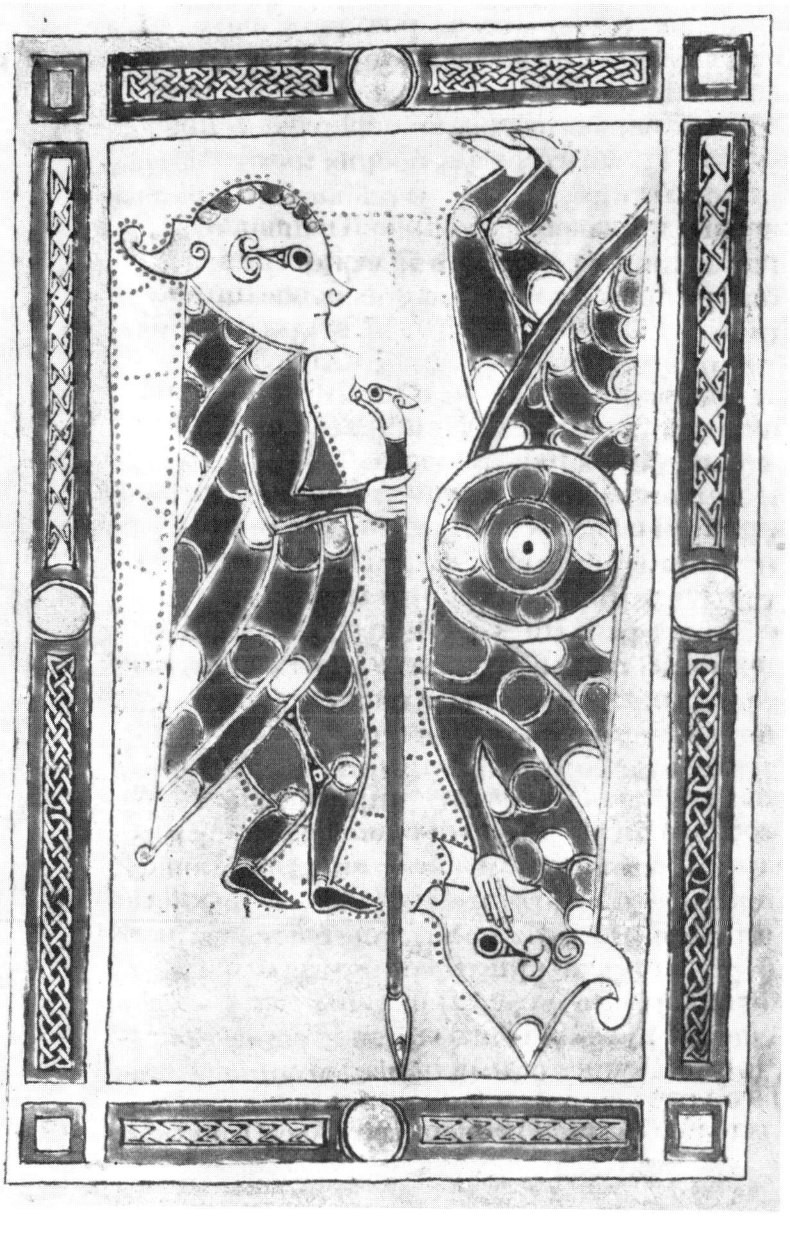

'Southampton Psalter'
Ms. C. 9, David and Goliath

author and singer of psalms and by the particular type of shepherd's staff which he carries. David is shown holding a similar kind of staff in two psalter illustrations of the 10th and 11th century. In the earlier of the two, the Cotton Psalter, the comparison is particularly close in the scene where David, holding the short staff, confronts Goliath. The shepherd's staff alluding as it does to David's deliverance of the lamb from the lion also refers to David's role as a prefiguration of the role of Christ the Saviour. The same double interpretation is reflected in the Lord of Hosts scene on the tall cross at Monasterboice where the armed Christ is shown holding a similar animal-head staff.

Helen Roe, quoted by Ettlinger, was near to the truth when she interpreted the gesture towards the mouth as an indication of language, of the *spoken* word. As well as referring to David's role as psalmist the same gesture could illustrate a recurrent theme in David's psalms, expressed thus in Psalm 5:- 'Give ear to my words, O Lord; give heed to my groaning. Hearken to the sound of my cry . . .'

In the Book of Samuel (1, 17, 40), the scriptural source for the psalter illustrations, David is described as going into battle against Goliath wielding only his shepherd's staff and a sling. In a small bag he had collected five stones as ammunition for his sling. This bag of stones may be the object suspended from the waist of the White Island David. An alternative interpretation is that this represents David's sling. David's hair-style, if it is one and not a cap, helmet or crown, is unlike that of any of the other statues. It is a fringed style with an unusual gap in the middle which leaves the forehead bare. It has been interpreted, without a great deal of evidence, as an Irish form of tonsure.

Scenes from the life of David were common in European Christian art, on early wall paintings, frescoes, stone carvings metal-work as well as in manuscripts. Most of the illustrations in continental and English Psalters were inspired by such themes. The Master of White Island very probably derived inspiration for this carving from contemporary Irish psalters. It is not surprising that he should choose to portray David. Symbolising as he does God's power to deliver the faithful from their enemies, David's image must have inspired hope and trust in a community subject to the terrors of Viking raids.

Ettlinger, E, *Ogam,* 10, 1958, 267.

14(f) **Statue with Bell and Crozier. St Anthony of the Desert or Christ Abbot of the World?**
Height of stone 105cm; Height of statue 92.5cm; Width 33cm; Thickness 24cm.
Socket: Width 12.5cm; Length 20.5cm (to wall); Depth 1.5cm.

This was found in 1958 in the lowest course of the 12th century church wall. The veil-like hood worn by this figure has led at least one writer to suggest that this is a nun or abbess. A more likely interpretation, given the episcopal emblems of bell and crozier held by the figure, is that the hood identifies the subject either as a travelling abbot or bishop (Christ Abbot of the World?) or as an anchorite abbot or bishop. (The episcopal emblems pertained to abbots as well as to bishops in the early Irish Church.) If the subject is an anchorite it could be St Anthony of the desert, first of the abbots, and be intended as a commemoration of the origins of Irish monasticism in the anchorite movements of Egypt. St Anthony was a popular subject on contemporary High Crosses and was most commonly depicted on his visit to St Paul in the desert. On Muiredach's cross at Monasterboice Paul and Anthony are shown holding crooked croziers like the one on this statue. It has also been suggested that the subject of this statue was a local saint, an 8th century anchorite and abbot, Constans of Eo-Inis. But because White Island has not been certainly identified with Eo-Inis this attribution is for the moment untenable. St Anthony or Christ, unlike Constans, are subjects of wider import and as such would be more in keeping with the universal symbolism of the other statues. The title Abbot of the World is given to Christ in some Irish texts.

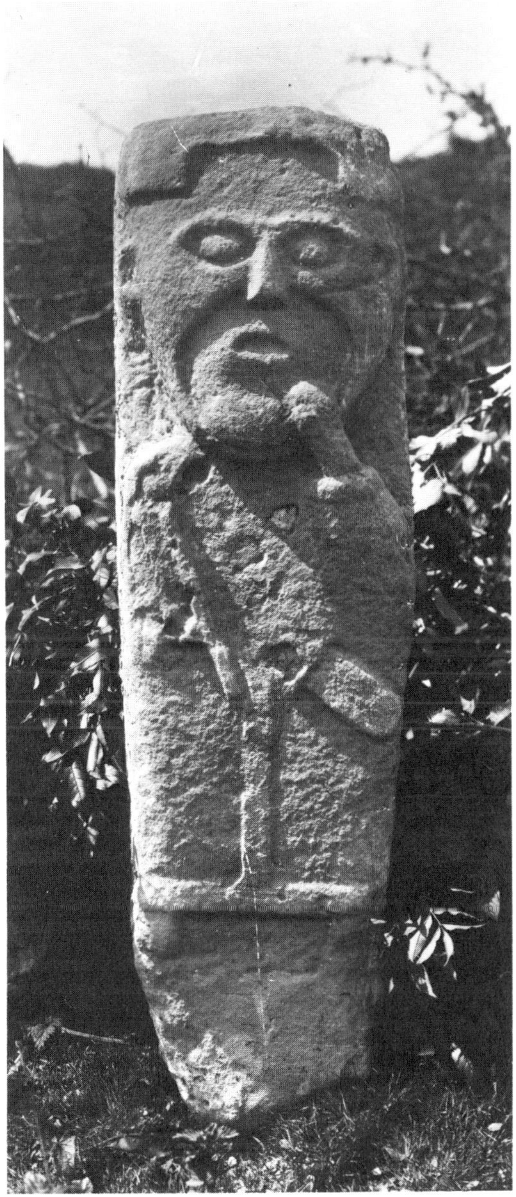
14(e)

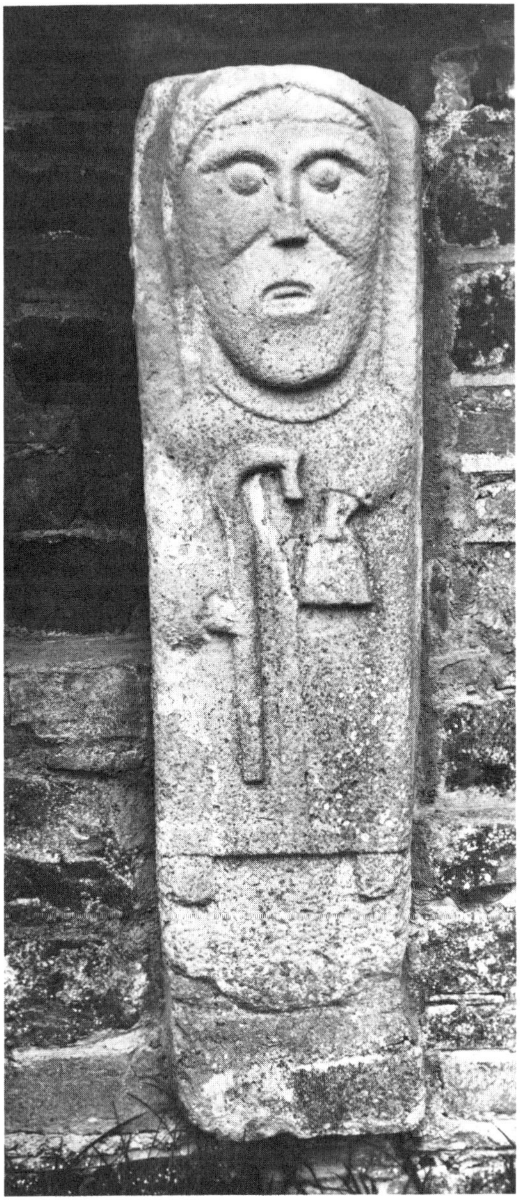
14(f)

The crooked crozier provides another clue to the dating of these statues. Metal enshrined croziers of this shape were common in Ireland in the 9th, 10th and 11th century. This statue has a longer narrower face than the other statues and a neater appearance probably due to the ears being hidden from view by a shoulder-length hood. Two small bulges in the stone at knee level suggest that the subject is seated.

Rogers, M, *Prospect of Erne*, 1967, 71-72.
Henry, F, *Irish Art during the Viking Invasions 800-1020 AD*, 1967, Fig 40 (a).
Lowry-Corry, Lady D, *Ulster J Arch*, 1959, 61-63.

15 **Carved Head on White Island**

This head is carved on a large slab (Length 55.8cm; Width 40.6cm). It was found with other statues and the unfinished piece in 1928, built into the east gable of the 12th century church. It resembles the statue heads except in its scowling expression. Although it is often considered to be later than the statues — a medieval copy? — its use as building material in the church wall makes this unlikely. Its superficial resemblence to medieval carved heads is probably fortuitous and it seems best to regard it as being from the same atelier as the statues.

Lowry-Corry, Lady D, *Ulster J Arch*, 1959, 59-61.

16 **Carved Pillar ('Bishop's Stone') Killadeas Graveyard, Co Fermanagh**
Height 82cm; South side Width 41cm; West side Width 23 cm.

The bishop or abbot is carved in low relief on the South side. He is shown in profile walking westward and carrying the same episcopal emblems of bell and crozier as are shown on one of the White Island statues. On the narrow west side of the pillar a crudely carved human face stands out in bold relief above a panel of broad-ribbon interlacing. The top of the pillar has been chipped away, defacing the carvings on both sides.

Controversy about date of Pillar
The two sides of this pillar are carved in very different styles, the high relief treatment of the face providing a sharp contrast to the false relief of the ecclesiastic. A close examination of the face reveals that part of its left cheek has been cut off and straightened. This was done as a result of the carving of the ecclesiastic on the other dressed side and undoubtedly means that the face was the earlier of the two carvings. How much earlier is in question.

The controversy stems from the suggestion that the face belonged to a 'Celtic' idol and that the carving of the ecclesiastic was designed to 'christianize' this pagan monument. The case for a pagan origin is weak and a more plausible case exists for accepting the two sides of the pillar as roughly contemporary work of the 9th, 10th or possibly 11th century.

Although the face has the remote expression found on the pagan idol from Boa Island, the actual details of the features — the round bulbous eyes, the open mouth with protruding lips and the rounded cheeks and chin — compare far more closely with the White Island statues than with pagan sculpture. As for the difference in carving style, the same combination of flat and higher relief carving exists on other Early Christian monuments, notably on the two pillars form Carndonagh, Co Donegal, where both styles are almost certainly contemporaneous.

There are other indications — the presence of the bell and crozier emblems, the use of the same

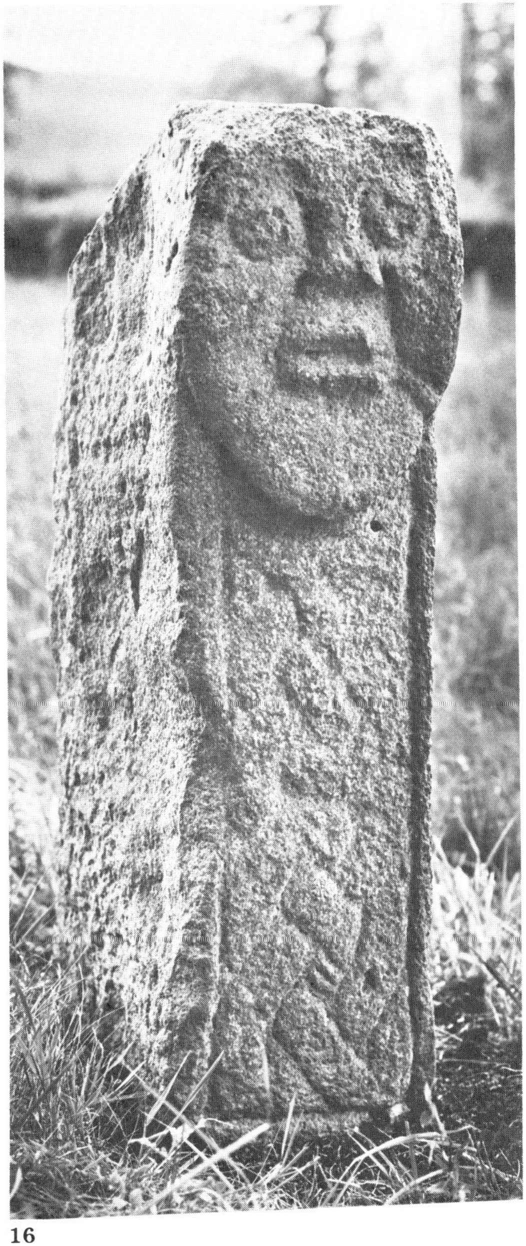

16

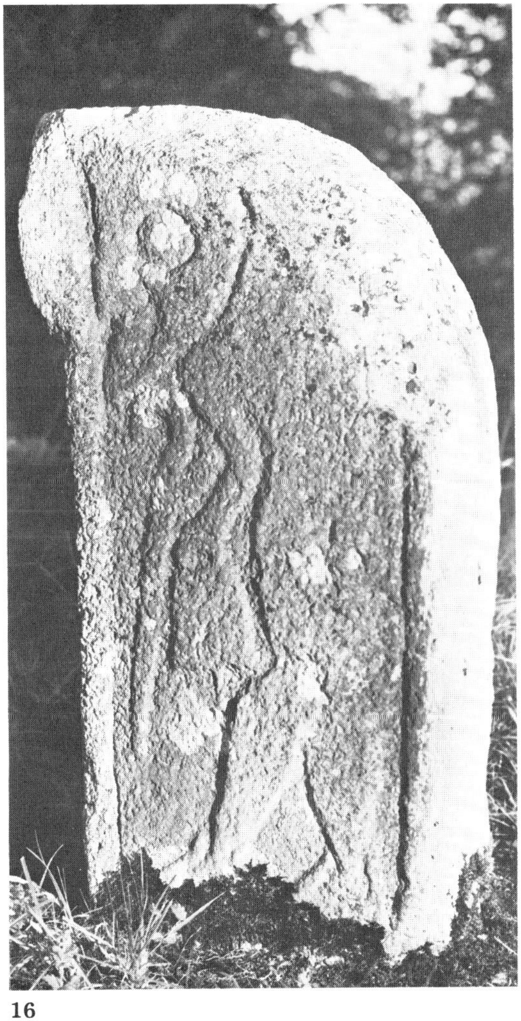

16

kind of interlaced motif — which point to close connections between the White Island statues and this pillar. The latter may even have started out as an attempt by a less skilled stone-carver to copy the work of the Master of White Island. This would account for the similarities between the high relief Killadeas face and the faces of the statues. Perhaps the carver found it too difficult to reproduce the three dimensional quality of the White Island models and opted for finishing the pillar in the low relief style to which he was more accustomed.

The flat figure of the walking abbot or bishop was probably modelled on some manuscript illustration. His shoes have a peculiar carved outline which is very reminiscent of the way shoes in manuscript illuminations are outlined in different colours. (See Southampton Psalter, David and Goliath.) The somewhat caricaturish treatment of his face, with bulging eye and exaggeration of chin and nose, is very like that of the profiled drawings of David in the 10th century Cotton Psalter and in the early eleventh century Southampton Psalter.

Macalister identified an inscription 'Robartach' along the bishop's body but no trace of it survives. Neither are there any records of an abbot named Robartach from this area. It is more likely that this figure, like the White Island statue with bell and crozier, is to be identified as a subject of universal Christian import such as Christ Abbot of the World or St Anthony of the desert.

The name Killadeas probably derives from Céli-Dé (servants or companions of God). The Céli-Dé or Culdees originated in a reform movement within the monasteries in the 8th century. Sometimes a group of Céli-Dé lived austerely and in seclusion on the outskirts of a large monastery. Killadeas is believed to be the site of a Culdee foundation which was an offshoot of St Molaise's monastery on nearby Devenish Island.

Apart from the 'Bishop's Stone', there are several other interesting carved stones in Killadeas graveyard. These include two cross-slabs and a rounded pillar which may be a pagan phallic stone.

Lowry-Corry, Lady D, *J Roy Soc Antiq Ireland,* 65, 1935, 26-33, Pl VI.
Rynne, E, *C B A Research Report,* 9, 1972, 86.
Rogers, M, *Prospect of Erne,* 1967, 48-49, 139-140.

Romanesque Figure Carving

12th century AD

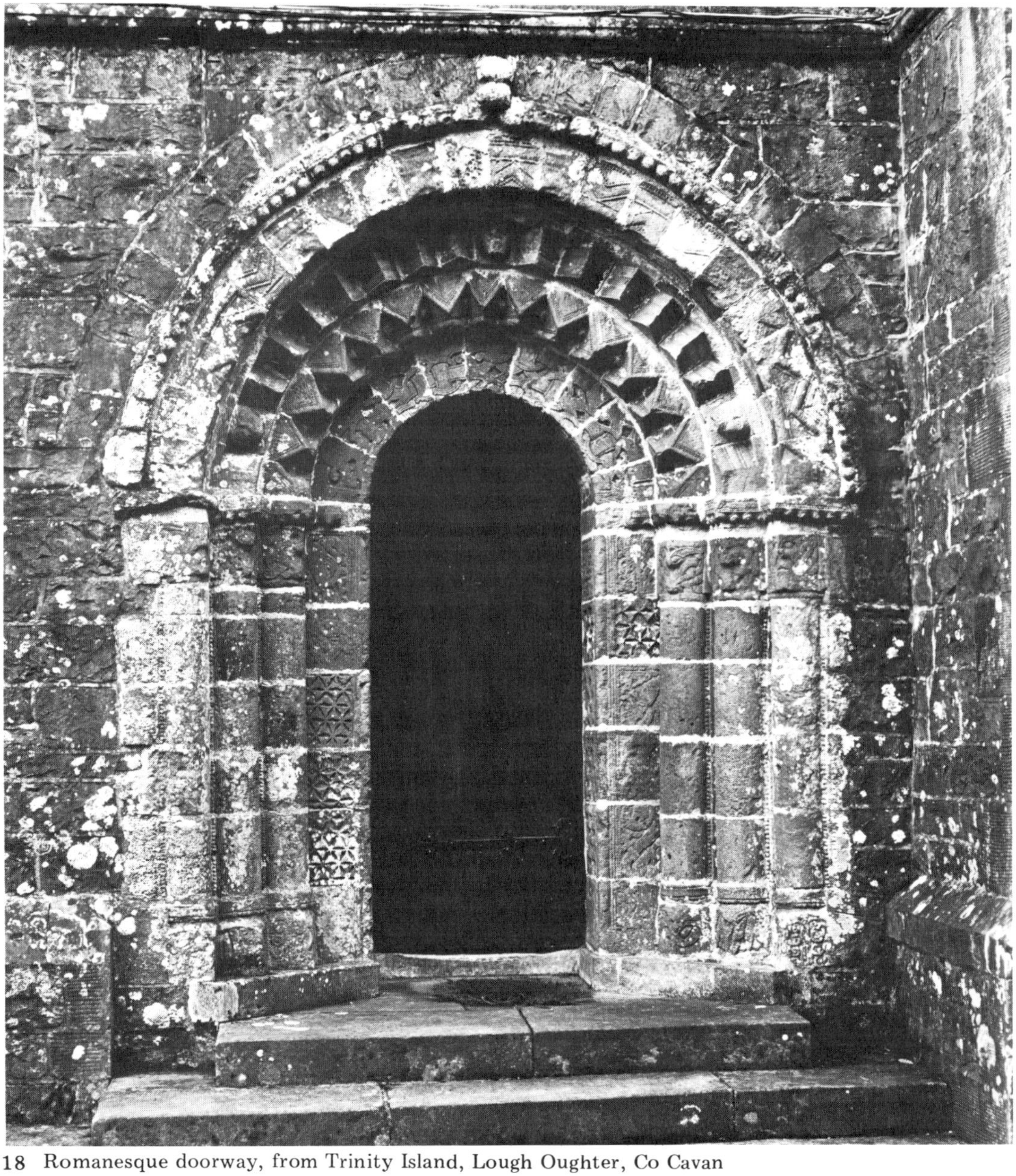

18 Romanesque doorway, from Trinity Island, Lough Oughter, Co Cavan

Romanesque is the term used to describe a type of building derived from the structural forms of Classical Rome. This architectural style first appears on the Continent about the middle of the 10th century in northern Italy and the Rhone valley where at that time extensive remains of Roman imperial buildings had survived. There was a marked increase in building activity throughout the Continent during the late 10th and 11th century when many of the timber-roofed churches destroyed by the Normans were replaced by elaborately designed stone-vaulted and domed structures.[1] The impact of this new architectural style was certainly felt in Ireland in the 12th century but, with the exception of Cormac's Chapel at Cashel, it resulted in small stylistic changes rather than in elaborate architectural innovations. In other words Irish Romanesque is more a decorative than an architectural style.

The most common decorative innovation was the round-arched doorway, a good example of which is found at Kilmore Cathedral in Cavan. This was often matched by a rounded chancel arch frequently built as part of a chancel addition to an existing church. Less common are decorative mouldings such as the cornice from Devenish Round Tower and the unusual carved figure, probably part of a gable-coping or a cornice, from Aghalurcher in Fermanagh. Round-arched windows were fairly frequently ornamented with abstract designs but the figure-carving on the window fragment from Berrymount in Cavan is quite exceptional. The carving of a bishop from Aghalurcher may originally have been set into the wall of the church perhaps arranged under arcading like the panels of Ardmore Cathedral, Co Waterford which contain carvings of bishops as well as biblical scenes.

Irish Romanesque Ornament

The hybrid nature of Irish Romanesque decoration is well known. It comprises elements drawn from English and Continental art as well as from Scandinavian and traditional Irish styles. The resulting combination of designs — chevrons, pellets, foliage, animal heads and many other motifs — quickly take on a distinctively Irish character.

In this regional survey we are concerned with only one Romanesque motif, namely the human figure and more particularly the human head. Arches with human heads are fairly common in Ireland and are believed to be the result of contacts with France and north-west Spain. The design probably originated in the Near East and appeared early in French Romanesque art.[1] Its relative popularity in Ireland contrasts with its rarity in England where it is superseded by a closely related motif — the arch with animal heads. The three radially placed heads on the Kilmore arch in Cavan are good examples of the Irish style and resemble French examples such as the bearded heads on the cloisters of the Benedictine Abbey of St Aubin at Angers.[3] Heads are not confined to arches but are also adapted for the decoration of capitals and cornices where the characteristic Irish treatment of the motif takes the form of elaborate interlaced patterns woven from the beards and hair of mask-like faces.

Irish Links with Western Europe

Borrowings from Continental Romanesque are seen as the result of renewed contacts between Ireland and Western Europe in the 11th and 12th century. These came about largely through the voyages of Irish pilgrims to Rome and to the tomb of St James of Compostella in north-west Spain. Some links between Irish and Continental monasteries must also have been maintained, particularly the long established links with those continental monasteries originally founded by Irish monks. There is also evidence for new Irish foundations abroad during this late period.

Pilgrimages

The pilgrim routes to Compostella, whether by land across England or direct by sea to France, meant passing through areas of France where arches with human and animal heads could be seen. The fact that the Irish distribution of arches with human heads is predominantly western suggests that there was an established pilgrim route from the West of Ireland to France, perhaps from the port of Limerick to a harbour on the Saintonge coast. From Saintonge the pilgrims could go either southwards towards Compostella or across the south of France towards Rome.[4] There was probably another route to Rome across the north of France and through Burgundy. An Irish pilgrim on this route may have brought the Irish Psalter of St Ouen to the monastery of St Evroult near Argentan in Normandy in the 11th or early 12th century.[5]

The pilgrimages of Irish rulers to Rome are frequently mentioned in the Annals during the 11th century. This information takes on added significance when one recalls that much of the church building and the production of fine metalwork during this and the following century was due to the patronage of such chieftains. The pilgrimages to Compostella were also probably taking place at this time although the earliest reference to that pilgrimage is not until the early 13th century when a hostel was built in Dublin to accommodate pilgrims awaiting boats. This reference suggests that it was a popular and well-established pilgrimage by that date. The recent discovery in Dublin of 12th century pottery from northern France suggests that commercial links may also have contributed to the flow of artistic ideas from France.

Romanesque Exhibitionist Figures

Two of the most unusual Romanesque carvings are the male exhibitionist figures on the Aghalurcher stone and the Berrymount window fragment. The two have a lot in common. Both have large heads with prominent ears, both lack bodies and phallus, and in both cases the testicles are shown next to the buttocks. These are the only examples of male exhibitionist figures from Ireland and a new term 'Seamus na mogairle' has been invented to distinguish them from the better known female equivalents — 'Sheila-na-gigs'.

The term 'Sheila-na-gig', probably an anglicization of the Irish Síle na gcíoch (Sheila of the paps) is usually used to describe medieval (ie post Norman) carvings of women displaying exaggerated genitalia. However at least one example of an earlier 'Sheila' is known from Ireland, on one of the voussoirs of the Romanesque chancel arch in the Nun's Chapel, Clonmacnoise. This and the Aghalurcher figure are depicted in remarkably acrobatic and distorted poses illustrating what seems to be a peculiarly Romanesque treatment of the subject.

Origin?

Female exhibitionist figures occur in a Romanesque context in France and England as well as in Ireland. The male types are apparently confined to France and Ireland. Two separate studies of these figures are at present being prepared for publication by Anthony Weir of Belfast and Jorgen Andersen of Denmark. These will include surveys of English and French examples and should throw some light on the many problems posed by these carvings.

If the Romanesque exhibitionist figures of both sexes are grouped together the Irish examples may be seen to follow closely the distribution of Romanesque arches with human and animal heads for which a French or Spanish origin has be claimed. Despite the small number of examples — only three — this distribution may be of significance, particularly in view of the absence of 'Seamus-na-mogairles' in Britain. The number of French exhibitionist figures of Romanesque style is not yet known but it does include at least one 'Seamus'.[6] In Britain at least six Romanesque 'Sheilas' are known, one of which, at Whittlesford in Cambridgeshire, is associated with a male monster.[7]

If a survey of French exhibitionist figures reveals close similarities between French and Irish examples, the likelihood is that the idea behind these strange carvings germinated in France and reached Ireland along with other Romanesque motifs. However the possibility that the traffic of ideas was in the opposite direction should also be considered.

Irish Origin?

The strongest case for an Irish origin of Sheila-na-gigs rests with the two female carvings discussed in the last chapter — the partially naked statue on White Island and the splay-legged figure on the Monasterboice cross. These figures were almost certainly used to illustrate some Christian theme. But in a wider sense they could be regarded as expressions of Irish ideas about the demoniacal powers of womenkind. Ideas such as these may, along with the actual sculptural images, have played some part in the creation of the exhibitionist motif in Romanesque carving. However no comparable male figures exist to account for the early origins in Ireland of Romanesque 'Seamus-na-mogairles'.

Anne Ross takes this idea of an Irish origin for 'Sheilas' one step further with her suggestion that 'Sheilas' are representations of the hag-like aspects of 'Celtic' territorial or war goddesses.[8] These are frequently referred to in the early Irish tales and are noted for their powers of sexuality and fecundity. They appear in the tales in single or triple form as repellent creatures with exaggerated genitalia. This theory, however, is considerably weakened by the absence of 'Sheila-na-gigs' in any datable context prior to the 9th or 10th century.

Summary of Exhibitionist figures:- The question of the origins of exhibitionist figure-carving is a highly complex one. In the Romanesque period, male and female types are known both in France and Ireland. Earlier female exhibitionist carvings are known in Ireland. In the following chapter some later Sheila-na-gigs will be discussed as well as the functions of all the different types.

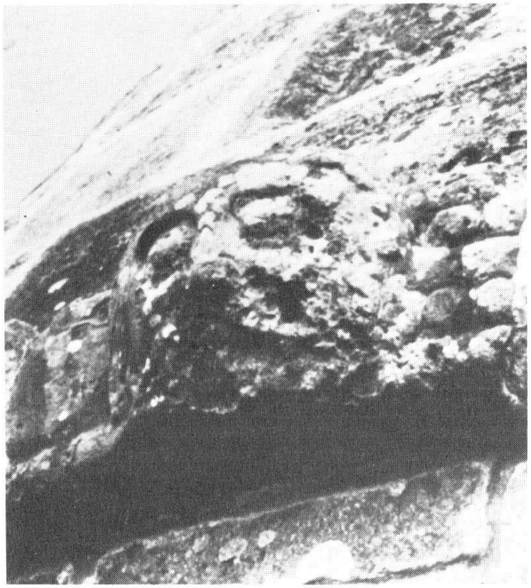
17

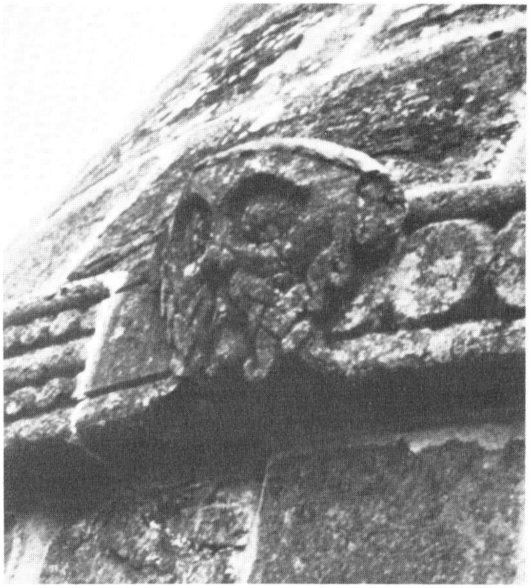
17

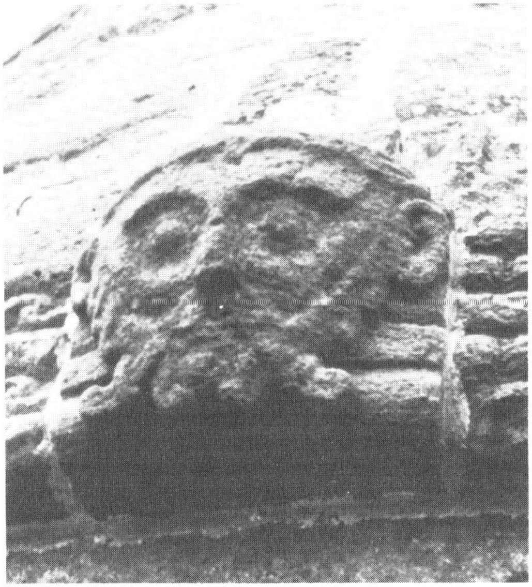
17

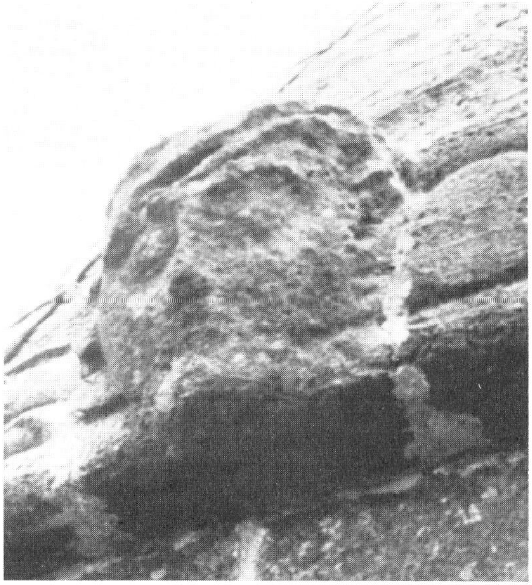
17

17 **Carved Heads on Cornice of Round Tower, Devenish, Co Fermanagh**

The cornice decorates the top of the tower wall just below the conical roof. Four carved heads face the four cardinal points while the intervening sections of the cornice have bands of pellets, either single or double, and interlocking s-curves. The heads, all slightly different, have flattened mask-like faces, two of them with beard and moustache arranged as an interlaced pattern. One of the heads is beardless. The fourth has side locks and a moustache. Its chin is badly defaced and may originally have been bearded. One view is that these heads represent local Irish saints. The beardless one is thought to be a woman, St Brigid or the local St Fancha of Rossory, the other three Molaise, Patrick and Columba. Another view is that they represent the four Evangelists, with John the youngest being shown without a beard.

The ornament on the cornice is of mid 12th century type and provides a date for the building of the Round Tower. This tower and the nearby St Molaise's Oratory show that the Romanesque stone-work on Devenish was of a particularly high quality. A reference in the 'Annals of Ulster' to the burning of Devenish in 1157 AD has led to the suggestion that the work of rebuilding began about 1160 AD. The Round Tower probably replaced an earlier tower, the foundations of which were recently excavated beside the present tower.

Ralegh Radford, C A, *Ulster J Archaeol,* 33, 1970, 57-8.
Waterman, D M, *Ulster J Archaeol,* 36-37, 1973-74, 100-102.
McKenna, Rev J E, *Devenish,* 1931, 47.

18 **Romanesque Doorway from Trinity Island, Lough Oughter, Co Cavan. Reconstructed at Kilmore Cathedral, Co Cavan**

Around 1860 the doorway was built into the vestry on the north side of Kilmore Church of Ireland Cathedral. It is said to have been taken from the Abbey on Trinity Island for use as the south door of the 17th century Cathedral of Kilmore. The Abbey on Trinity Island was a Premonstratensian foundation of 15th century date. Its builders probably reused the earlier Romanesque portal as a west doorway. Nothing is known of the church in which it was first used, nor is it certain that this church was on Trinity Island. The doorway, made of limestone and sandstone, is not correctly restored, which is not surprising when one recalls the number of times it has been dismantled.

The ornament of this doorway is typical of Irish Romanesque in the way its inspiration can be traced to widely differing sources. The probable French or Spanish inspiration for the three radially placed heads on the third order has already been mentioned. Scandanavian influences are apparent particularly in the animal ornament while the treatment of two of the capitals is typically Irish. The latter belong to the outer order and are in the form of human heads with eyebrows, moustaches and beards trailing off into three-strand interlacing.

The three human heads on the arch are symetrically arranged in a chevron design. Two of them have interlaced beards while the third, in the centre, is clean-shaven. All three have broken chins.

It has been suggested by Davies that the finial stone above the drip moulding of this doorway is a mutilated Sheila-na-gig but this is almost certainly incorrect. It looks very like an animal head biting the moulding underneath. This is a motif very characteristic of Romanesque carving. A date in the third quarter of the 12th century has been suggested for this doorway on account of its fully developed Romanesque style. However because of its remote situation it might be a bit later.

Davies, O, *J Roy Soc Antiq Ireland,* 78, 1948, 99-109.
Henry, F, *La Sculpture Irlandaise,* 1933, 81-82, 188-9, Pls 146-149; 152.

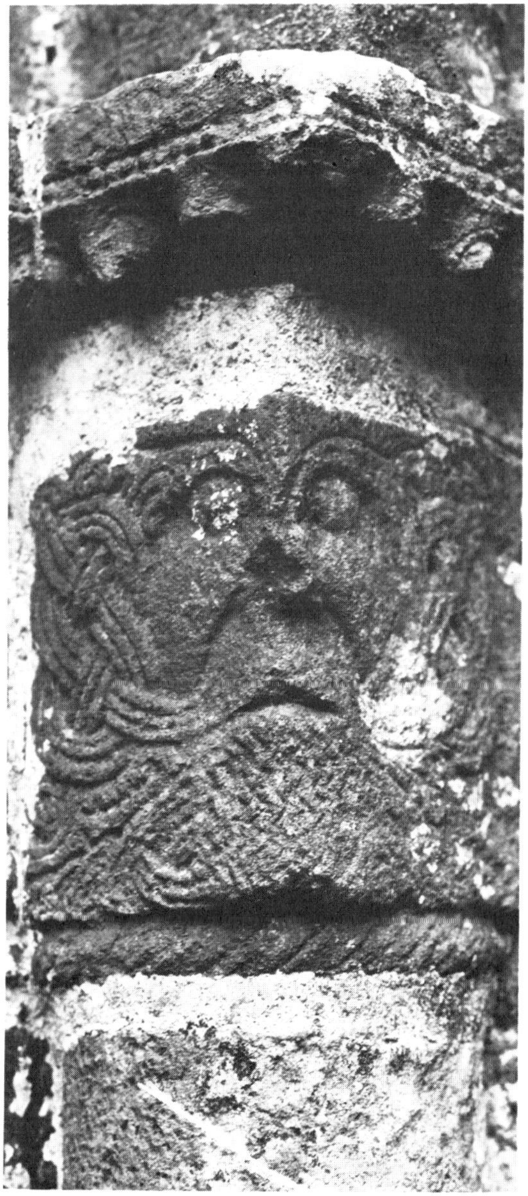
18

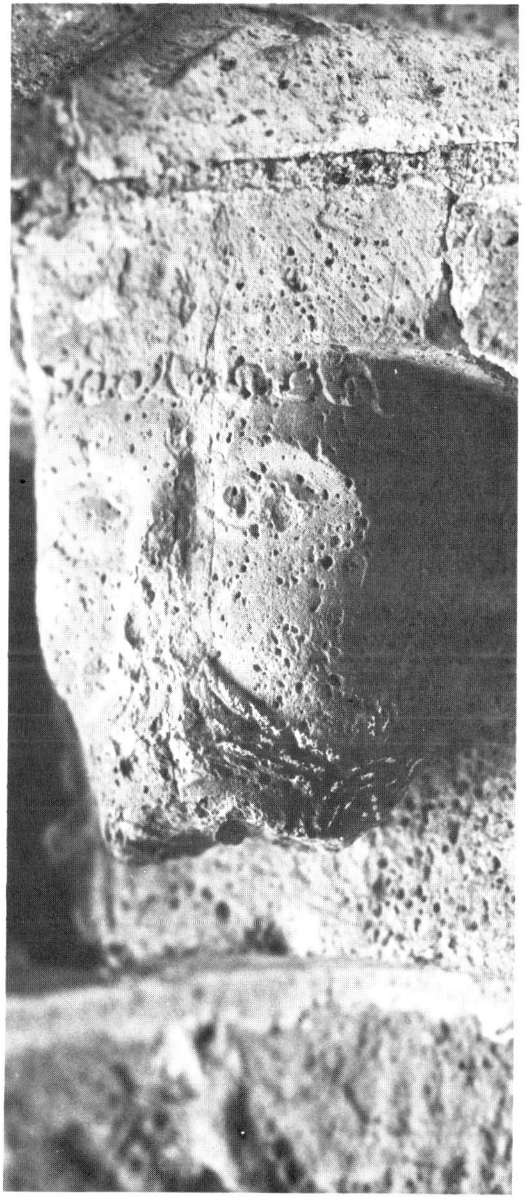
18

19 **Male Exhibitionist Figure on Romanesque Window, Berrymount, Co Cavan**
Now at Ballyconnell Church of Ireland Church, Co Cavan.
Height 58cm; Max Width 89cm; Thickness 33cm; Width of Window 21cm splaying to 34cm.

This very strange carving in sandstone consists of a long oval head with large staring eyes and animal-like ears centrally placed above an arched opening. A pair of arms with hands outstretched springs form both cheeks. The tips of the fingers are within reach of two biting beast-heads. Recessed below the bearded head and carved in lower relief is the cleavage of the buttocks between two legs shown in profile. The testicles are further recessed below this.

This carving was part of the outer face of a narrow, splayed, round-headed window, almost certainly Romanesque and probably, as Davies suggested, from a Round Tower rather than a church. The small size of the opening would be particularly appropriate for the window of a Round Tower.

Half a mile from the ditch in which this carving was found is the site of the early monastery of Toomregon (Tuaim Drecon) where traces of a church and Round Tower survive. In the 7th century the abbot of this monastery, St Briccene, was renowned fro his skill as a brain surgeon. He was responsible, according to legend, for healing the scholar Cenn Faelad who had been severely wounded at the battle of Mag Roth in 637 AD. According to the same legend Cenn Faelad, after his recovery, studied at the three schools of Toomregan — the school of Latin learning, Irish law and Irish poetry.

The survival of this legend has led to the misinterpretation of the beast heads on the Romanesque window. Several writers have described the beasts as stylized skulls or faces and have seen in them a reference to Briccene's work as a brain surgeon. The beast head on one side is slightly damaged but the second head can be clearly seen as a head in profile with its wide-open jaws revealing sharp teeth and a long tongue. Similar beast heads appear occasionally on Irish metal and stone work of the 12th century, for example on one of the jambs of the Dysert O'Dea doorway in Co Clare and on a shrine called the Breac Maodhóg from Drumlane in Co Cavan.

This motif of attacking beasts probably illustrated some Christian theme possibly that of man's struggle against evil. The genital display may have symbolized the nature of man's temptation but could also have fulfilled the function of averting evil. Anthony Weir believes this figure could represent a female rather than a male, and prefers to think of it as sexually ambiguous.

Davies, O, *J Roy Soc Antiq Ireland*, 78, 1948, 116-117 P1 XXI.
Dickie, K M, *J Roy Soc Antiq Ireland*, 93, 1963, 198-199.
Killanin, Lord and Duignan, M V, *The Shell Guide to Ireland*, 1967, 94.

20 **Male Exhibitionist Figure on Gable-coping or Cornice, Aghalurcher, Fermanagh**
Now at the Archaeological Survey, Department of the Environment, Belfast.
Depth of cornice 15cm. Under-side with figure: Depth 22cm; Width 27.5cm.

A very expressive face with big wide ears and mouth wide-open in stern disapproval. Below the bearded chin, barely distinguishable from the beard are the testicles and up-turned buttocks. The legs are raised in acrobatic fashion, heels touching ears.

This interesting figure is part of a cut stone, angled in such a way as to suggest that the figure formed the under-section of either a cornice or a gable-coping. A less likely possibility is that it was a corbel supporting either a corbel-table or a cornice. The reconstructed drawing shows the possible position of the stone (a) at the gable end of the cornice or (b) at the base of the gable-coping.

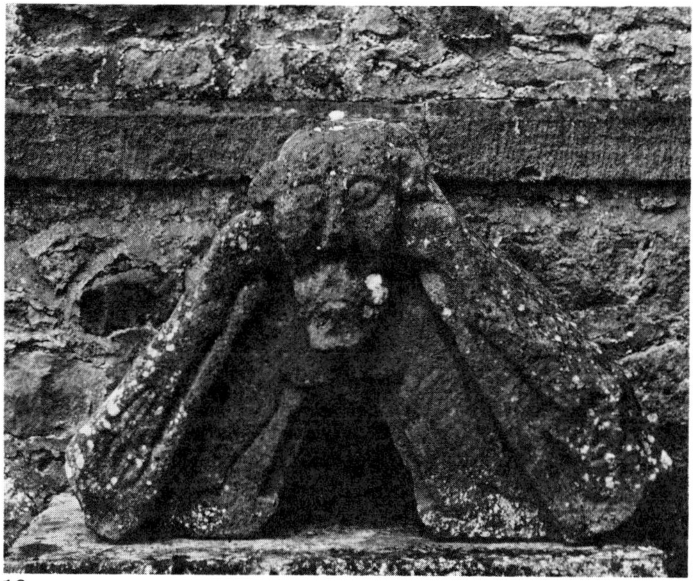

19

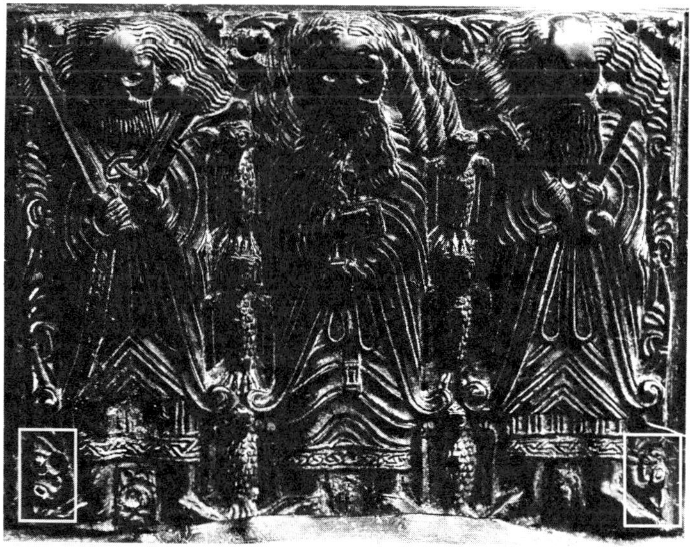

Breac Maodhóg from Drumlane, Co Cavan

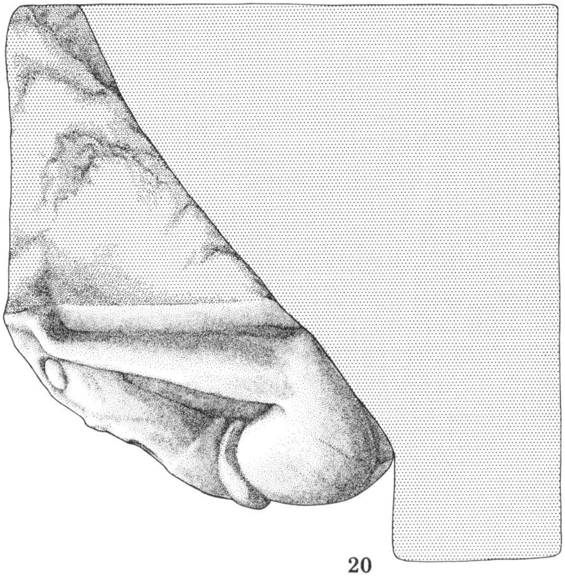

20

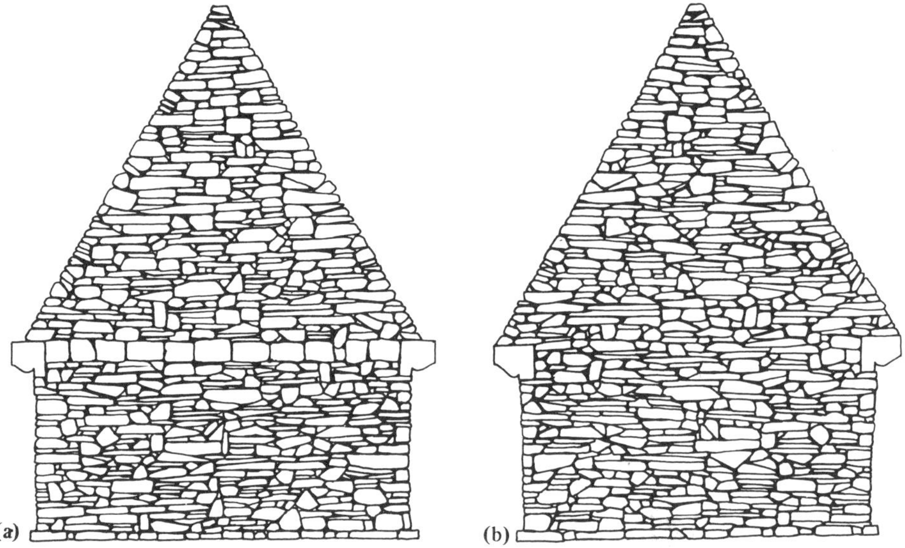

(a)

(b)

Possible positions of Aghalurcher figure:
(a) at the gable end of the cornice (ie part of a continuous moulded projection round wall);
(b) at the base of the gable coping (ie one of four such stones in a gabled church).

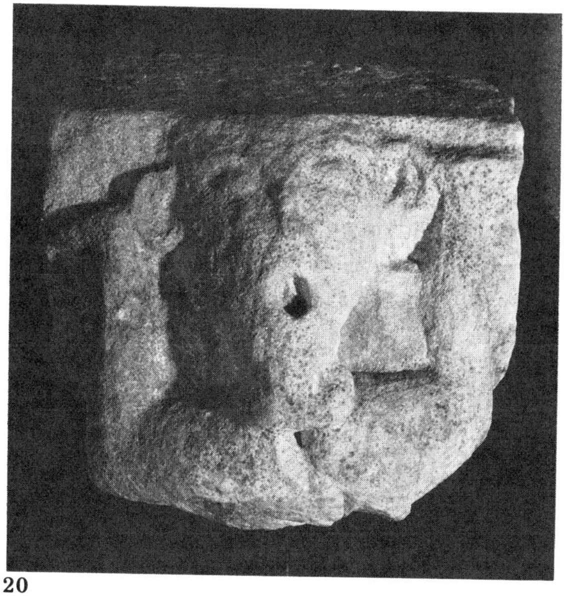
20

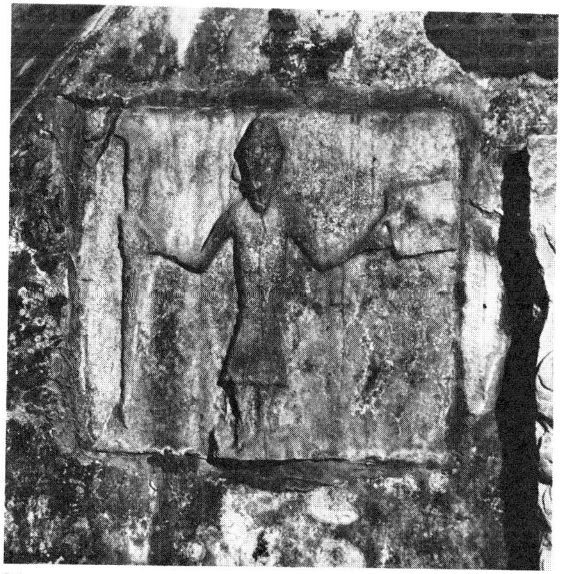
21

Cornices are occasionally found on Irish 12th century churches such as St Mochta's Oratory at Louth and Cormac's Chapel at Cashel, where they would have provided a measure of protection for walls, windows and doorways from the damaging effects of rain-water draining from the roof. In the Romanesque church at Guéron in Normandy obscene figures are carved on the undersection of the cornice.

In the course of restoration work by the Archaeological Survey, this stone was found built into the core of the south wall of Aghalurcher Church. The present ruins belong to a medieval church built on the site of an earlier monastery or church founded by the 7th century St Ronan. Nothing remains of the church, presumably Romanesque, to which this stone originally belonged.

21 **Figure of Bishop at Aghalurcher Church, Co Fermanagh**
Now set into wall of vault. Width 60cm; Height 55cm.

Only one side of the stone is dressed. This contains the full length relief carving of a bishop with outstretched arms holding a crozier and a square object. The shape of the latter suggests that it is either a metal shrine or possibly a leather satchel in which manuscript copies of the gospels were usually kept. The base of the crozier is sharply pointed and part of the crook has been broken. The bishop wears a conical mitre and a knee-length skirt. He has a long bearded face and wide ears. His feet rest on a semi-circular plinth which projects 6cm from the surface of the stone. Carvings of bishops are frequently found in the 12th century on High Crosses and Romanesque churches. They probably reflect the improved status of bishops resulting from the diocesan reforms of the period. It has been suggested that the conical mitre was instead a papal tiara and that these carvings of bishops were meant as representations of Christ as Abbot of the World. One of the best parallels for both the skirt and mitre of the Aghalurcher bishop is on the 12th century High Cross at Dysert O'Dea in Co Clare. The crucified Christ wears a pleated skirt while below him stands the mitred bishop.

This carving from Aghalurcher is known as the 'Bishop's stone'. In 1894 it was standing in the graveyard, apparently in use as a gravestone. It was believed to mark the grave of a 15th century bishop Roger or Ross Maguire who died in 1483 and was buried in St Ronan's Church at Aghalurcher. The fact that it can now be dated securely to the 12th century makes this association extremely unlikely.

Dagg, G A, *J Roy Soc Antiq Ireland*, 1894, 264-270.
Hunt, J, *Irish Medieval Figure Sculpture 1200-1600*, 1974, 1, 47.
Henry, F, *Irish Art in the Romanesque Period, 1020-1170 AD*, 1970, 139, P1 60.

The Medieval Period

Decorative Heads and other Carvings from Medieval Churches: 13th to 16th century

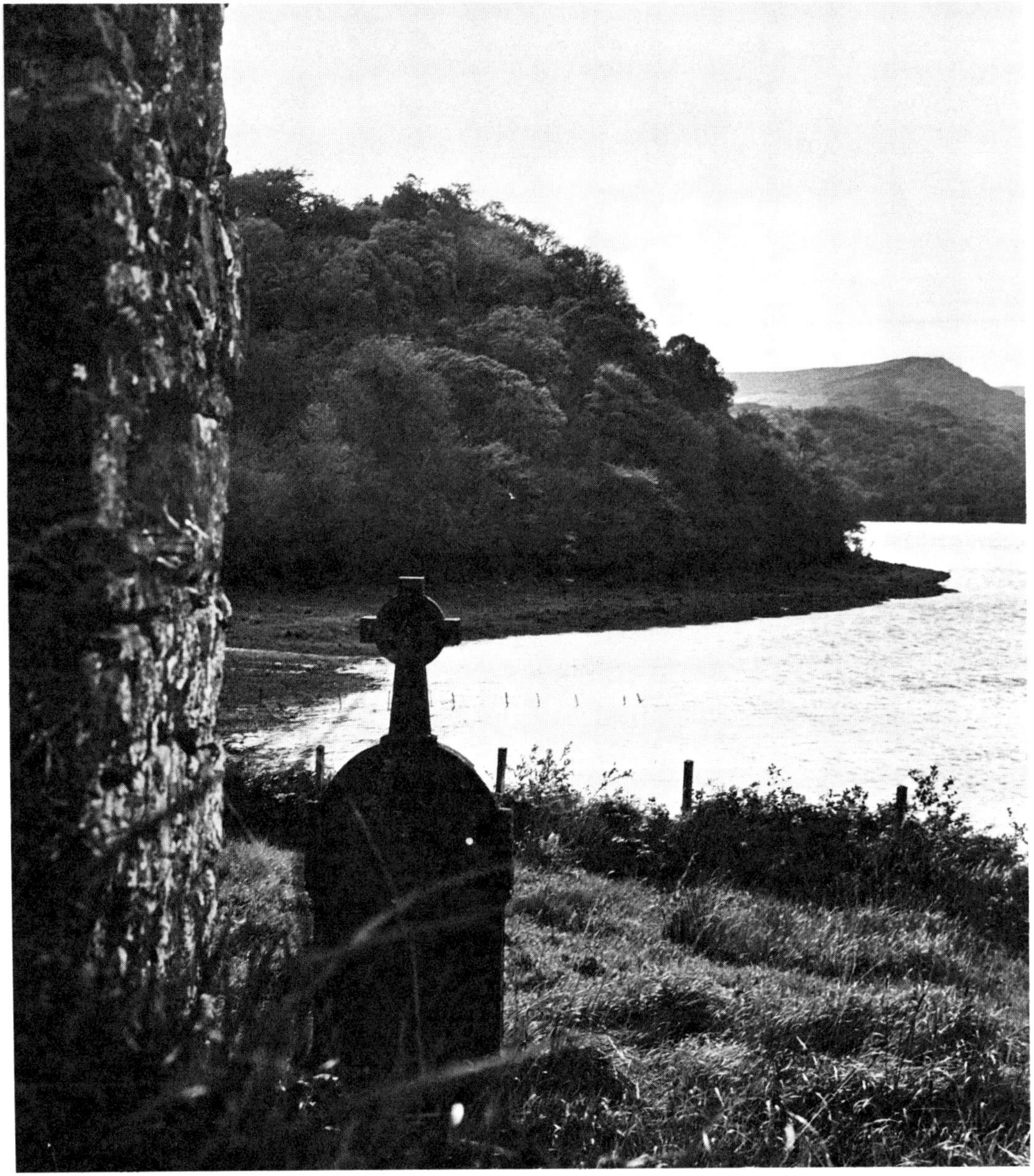

Carrick graveyard, Co Fermanagh

The failure of the Normans to successfully invade and colonize Fermanagh and Cavan contributed largely to the development of the Lough Erne area into a conservative and independant entity in the medieval period. At that time the Irish made no distinction between the Upper and Lower Lakes. Lough Erne for them stretched from about Belturbet to the falls of Assaroe beyond Belleek.[1] This area had always tended to be somewhat isolated. It was cut off from the seaport of Ballyshannon by the Assaroe falls at the mouth of the Erne, and by mountains from easy access to much of the neighbouring country. Most of the figure-carving of this period adorned abbeys and churches. Many of the latter, particularly in Fermanagh are small parish churches situated on islands or near the lough shore. They suggest a picture of busy waterways, particularly on Sundays and indicate the dependance of the population on water transport in medieval times. Many of these island churches maintained guest-houses which accommodated pilgrims on their way to and from the famous pilgrimage of Lough Derg in Donegal.

The absence of Norman settlement meant that the usual Norman parochial pattern, which consisted of building a church next to a castle in each small parish, was not introduced in the Lough Erne area. In Cavan and Fermanagh parish churches were built on the same sites as the Early Christian churches and were supported by the same monastic lands administered by erenaghs. Erenaghs in medieval times were clerical families who provided food and services for the support of priests and bishops and contributed to the upkeep of the churches. In earlier times the title erenagh usually referred to an abbot. The amount of church-lands farmed by the erenaghs in Fermanagh during the medieval period was as much as one-sixth of the county.[2]

Heads from Medieval Churches

The carved heads from these medieval churches demonstrate the conservatism and isolation of the Lough Erne area. Stone carvers trained in the traditional Gothic styles certainly worked in the region, Matthew O'Dubigan at Devenish and anonymous masons at the churches of Derrybrusk and Drumlane. But much more common are heads carved in archaic styles such as the Tievealough head (Illustration 40) or in distinctive local styles such as three of the Cavan heads (Illustrations 38, 41 and 42) which are characterized by a peculiar emphasis on furrows. Sometimes the stonecarvers took their inspiration from Romanesque sculpture as the two unprovenanced heads in Enniskillen (Illustration 39) show. This archaism is so persistent that were it not for the architectural associations of many of these heads, it would be extremely difficult to date them accurately. The head carving of this period varies as much in quality as it does in form, ranging from the poorly cut head at Templenaffrin (Illustration 47) to the powerful image at Clannaphilip (Illustration 42).

Many of these heads served as stops[3] on the hood moulding of windows and frequently represent bishops or kings. Others decorated the outer end of corbels[4] or gable copings.[5] A few may have been purely decorative and two of them are thought to have belonged to effigial tombs (Illustrations 30 and 31). The building and adornment of these medieval churches must be attributed to the patronage of the local ruling families such as the O'Flanagans, O'Reilly's and above all the Maguires. The latter are frequently mentioned in the Annals of Ulster as builders of churches, and the family is specifically named in connection with the restoration of Aghalurcher Church, a Maguire parish church.

'Sheila-na-gigs'

Two of the carvings of this period are of grotesque female figures of the 'Sheila-na-gig' type. They were probably built into the outer church wall but their function is far from clear. We have noted the existence of two comparable exhibitionist figures in the Early Christian Period when they appear to have had a Christian function, perhaps serving as warnings against the evils of the Flesh. In Romanesque ecclesiastical buildings they are frequently placed in such a position as to be away from the close scrutiny of the congregation. Many would view these as flashes of medieval humour, some as comic reminders of our origins.[6]

The medieval 'Sheila-na-gigs' are, as the two Cavan examples illustrate, more fearsome than humourous. They are often regarded as expressions of underlying pagan rather than Christian beliefs. In the famous epic the Táin Bó Cúalnge, Cú Chulainn was quelled by an army of 150 women led by their chieftainess Scannlach whose only weapon was their display of nakedness from which the boy Cú Chulainn had to avert his face.[7] Stories like this may have encouraged the belief that 'Sheilas' could ward off evil, a function usually attributed to them. Male exhibitionist figures were also believed to have protective powers, an ability to draw off the malevolent influence of the evil eye.[8] The exhibitionist form of these figures, male and female could also suggest that fertility powers were attributed to them.

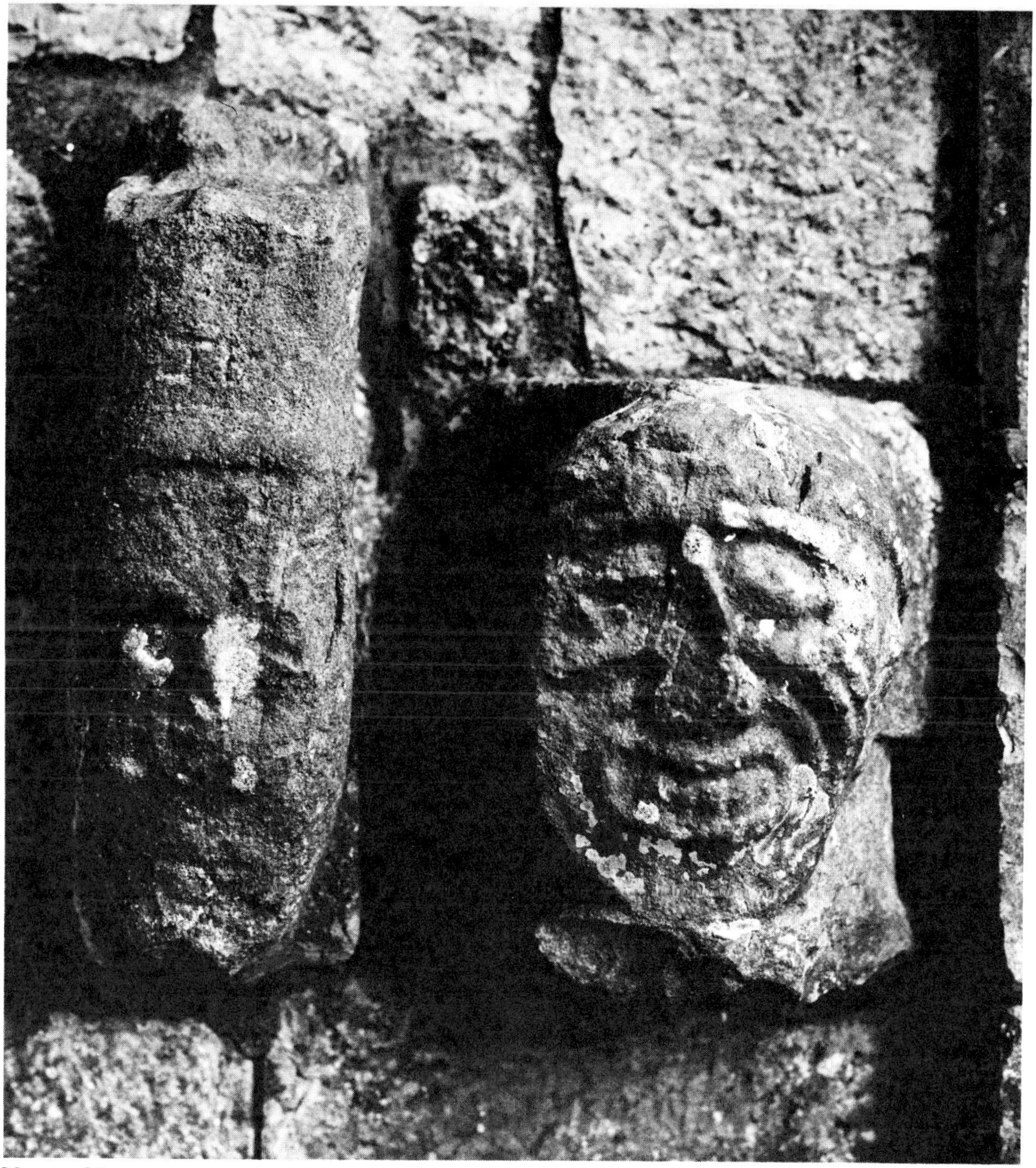

22 23

22 **Grotesque Head from St Molaise's Church? (Teampul Mor) Devenish, Fermanagh**
Now set in south wall of St Mary's Augustinian Priory, Devenish.
Max Width 23cm; Height 27cm.

According to Wakeman this head was found either inside or outside the ruined walls of St Molaise's church, a Transitional building of late 12th or early 13th century date with later domestic buildings. This was the parish church of Devenish in medieval times run by a community of secular priests knows as Culdees. The head may have been a mask-stop or corbel, but it is unlikely to be as early as the 13th century. It is made of sandstone and is rather crudely carved. The top and bottom are flat and the nose is broken. It has well defined ears and tonsure, a rounded chin and a very distinctive clownish mouth. It may have belonged to one of the buildings of the Augustinian Priory.

Wakeman, W F, *J Roy Soc Antiq Ireland*, 1880, 287, Fig 6.

23 **Bishop's Head at St Mary's Augustinian Priory, Devenish, Fermanagh**
Set in south wall under tower. Width 11.7cm; Height 35.5cm.

This has a elongated face and a high mitre the top of which is broken. It may have been a mask-stop or corbel and may have belonged to the same building as the grotesque head (Illustration 22). It is made of the same kind of sandstone.

These two heads (Illustration 22 and 23) are unlikely to have belonged to the Augustinian Priory church which is distinguished by its very fine 15th century carvings in millstone grit and limestone. They could perhaps have decorated a less important priory building such as the Chapter House. Although it has often been suggested that the Augustinian Priory was founded as early as the 12th or 13th century, neither the architectural nor the archaeological evidence supports this view. The evidence from recent excavations by Dudley Waterman in the area of the east range of Priory buildings did not suggest that these were earlier than the 15th century.

Mullarkey, T, *Clogher Record*, 4, 1960-61, 9-15.
Radford, C A Ralegh, *Ulster J Arch*, 33, 1970, 60-61.

24 **Coffin Lid from Graveyard of St Mary's Augustinian Priory, Devenish, Fermanagh**
Not illustrated.

This bears the very weathered carving of a human figure with rounded head and sloping shoulders. It is dated by Hunt to the late 13th or early 14th century.

Hunt, J, *Irish Medieval Figure Sculpture, 1200-1600*, 1974, 1, 147.

25 **Grotesque Head in site-museum Devenish, Co Fermanagh**
Width 20cm; Height 28cm; Thickness 7cm.

This crudely carved face on a thin irregularly shaped slab was found during recent restoration work on Devenish. It is probably a trial piece done by an unaccomplished stone-carver.

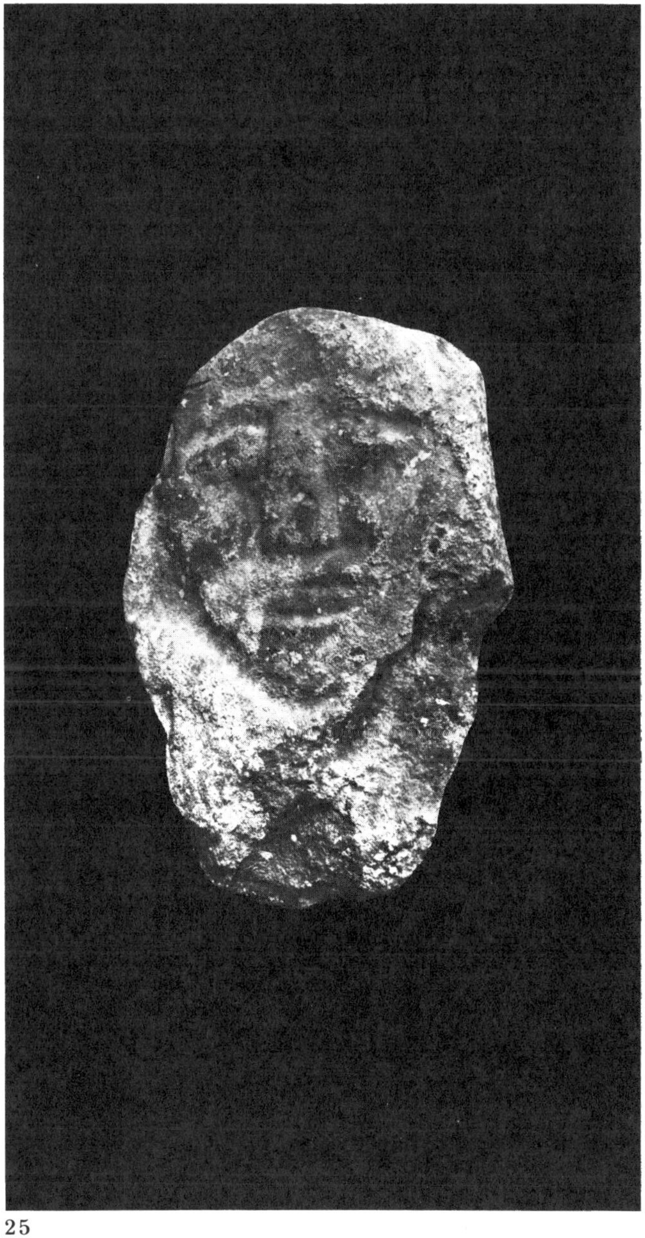
25

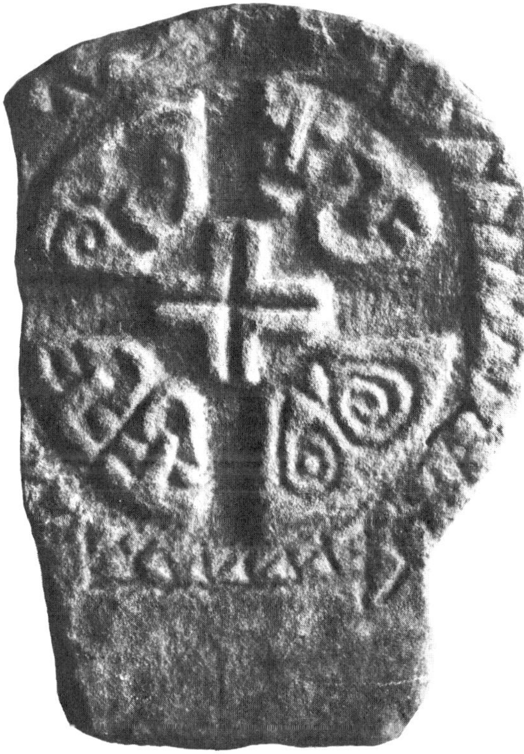
26

26 **Cross-slab at St Mary's Augustinian Priory, Devenish, Fermanagh**
Set in south wall under tower.

This very unusual cross-slab consists of a decorated circular head and a short shaft. In the centre of the head is a small equal-armed cross in false relief. In two opposing quadrants is carved a strange arrangement of two heads side by side. The other two quadrants contain simple scroll devices. A crudely carved zig-zag pattern forms a border around the circular head.

The cross-slab was removed from Devenish to Drumgay crannog near Enniskillen over a hundred years ago because the local farmer believed it had brought him bad luck. From there it was taken to Enniskillen where it was displayed for some time in a barber's shop. It is of uncertain date but is probably medieval.

McKenna, Rev J E, Canon, *Devenish*, 1931, 84.

27 **Head-finial from west door of St Mary's Augustinian Priory, Devenish, Fermanagh**
On display at site museum.

This well preserved and beautifully carved head-finial made of limestone was found during recent restoration work on the site. It probably represents the Virgin Mary, Queen of Heaven, shown with crown and flowing hair. The delicately carved features of the face are framed on either side by a single plait with out-turned ends. A noteworthy feature of the stone is the way the door mouldings on each side of the head vary in length. The west door may have been part of the work carried out by Matthew O'Dubigan in 1449. This work is commemorated by a Latin inscription on a stone in the church. It has also been suggested that this door was an early 16th century addition.

McKenna, Rev J E, Canon, *Devenish*, 1931, 68-71.
Mullarkey, T, *Clogher Record*, 4, 1960-61, 11.

28 **High Cross in Graveyard of St Mary's Augustinian Priory, Devenish, Fermanagh**

This High cross with its slender shaft and graceful open-work head is without parallel in Ireland. It is made of millstone grit, probably brought from Kesh in north Fermanagh. Above the crucifixion on the east side is a small bishop's head. On the narrow south side of the shaft a plait motif ends in an ogival arch above a small head in tranquil repose.

This elegantly carved cross can be dated by many of its motifs to the 15th century, for example its vine-leaves, ogival arches and cusps above and below the cross-arms. Parallels for some of its ornament, vine-leaves, plait and ogival arch, may be found on the elaborately carved ogee-hooded sacristy door in the north wall of St Mary's church which is also made of the same type of stone. The plait motif also turns up on the head-finial of the drip-moulding (Illustration 27) on the west door of this church.

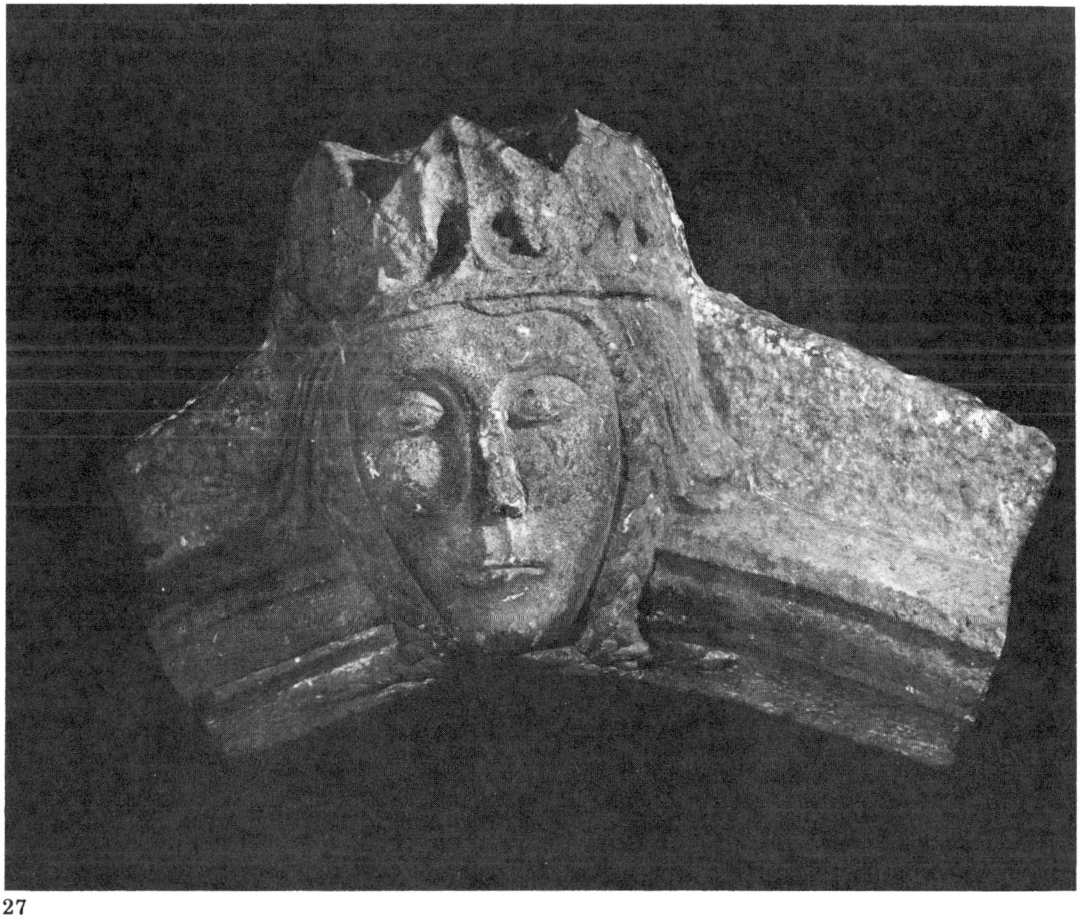

27

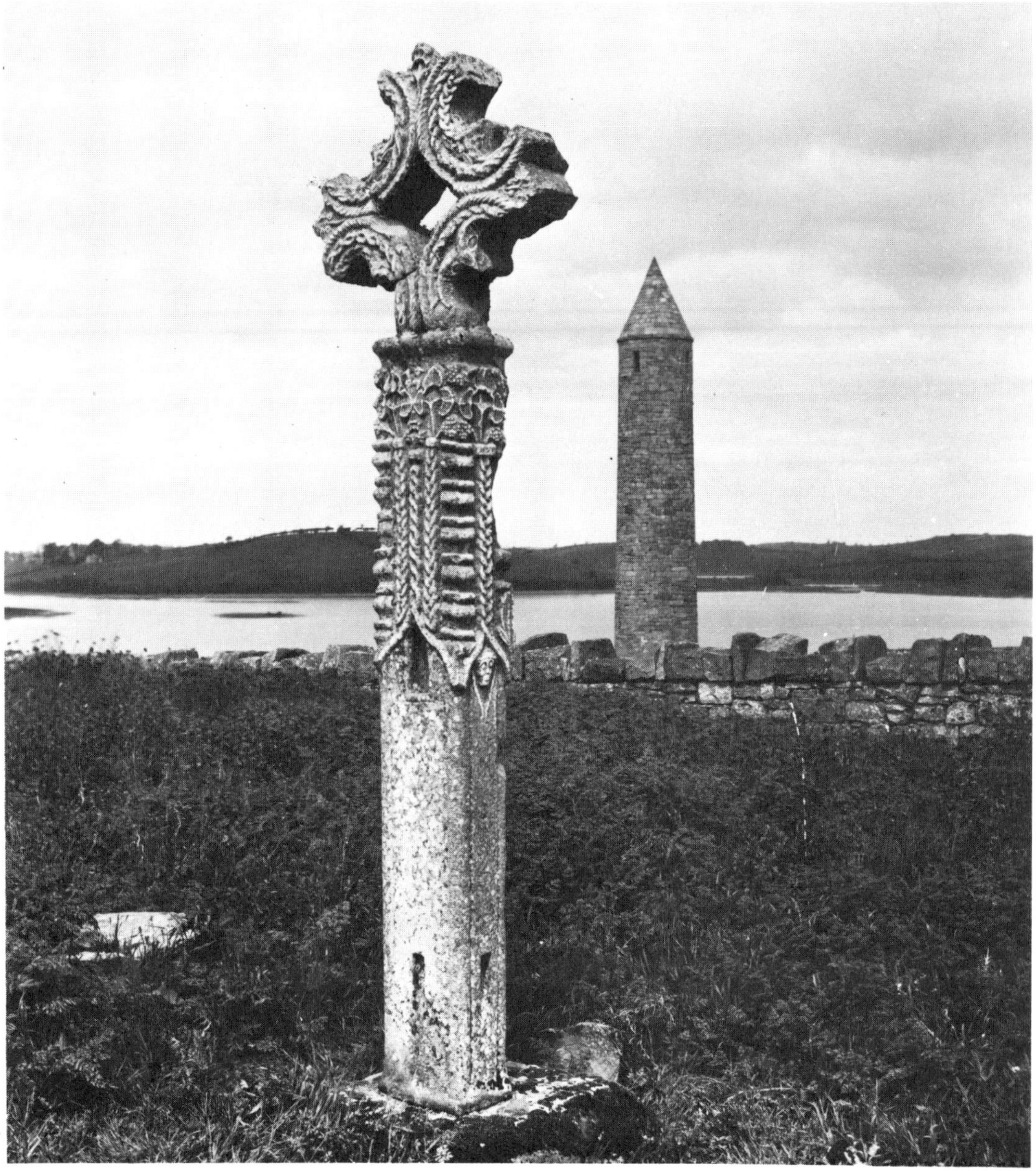

28

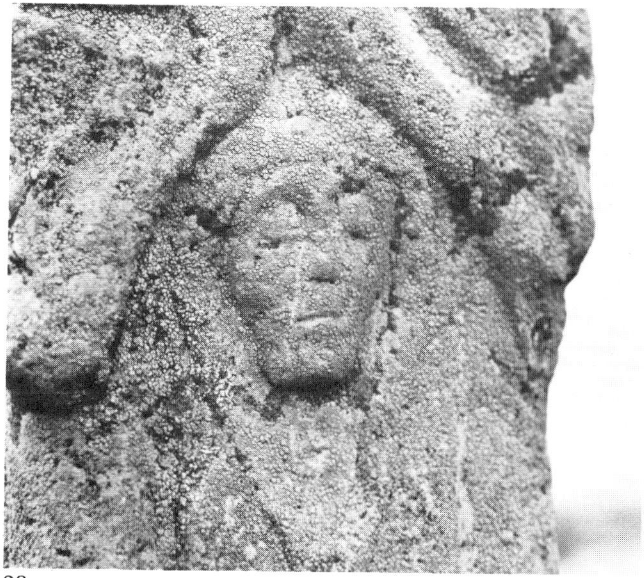
28

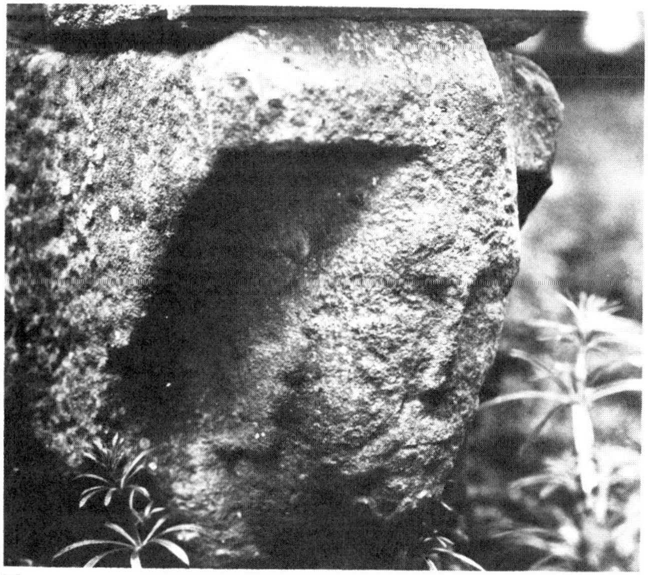
29

29 **Decorative Head on Gable-coping from Church on Cleenish Island, Fermanagh**
Width 26cm; Height 30cm; Depth 56.5cm.

This stone, possibly the base of a gable-coping, belonged almost certainly to the medieval parish church of St Sinell and not to the earlier stone church built here in 1100 AD ('Annals of Ulster'). In the 6th century a monastery was founded here by Sinell mac Mianaig, disciple of St Finian. There are two cross-slabs of Early Christian type lying in the graveyard. All that remains of the medieval church are numerous stones, many of them dressed, scattered about the graveyard. In 1790 the church and graveyard were despoiled of stones, head-stones and monumental slabs which were used to fill in the small arm of the lake where Enniskillen military barracks now stands.

The head, of weathered sandstone, stands out against a concave background. The expression on the face is one of repose and its features are finely carved in naturalistic manner. The curving hair-line on both sides suggests wavy hair. The top of the stone is not level. About half of it, immediately behind the head, has been carefully cut to form a shallow recess 18.5cm wide. This may have held the angled stone of the gable.

Rogers, M, *Prospect of Erne*, 1967, 103, 106.
Gwynn, A, and Hadcock, R N, *Medieval Religious Houses Ireland*, 1970, 31.

30,31 **Two Heads possibly from Cleenish, Fermanagh**
On loan to Enniskillen Museum from Mount Lourdes, Convent of Mercy, Enniskillen.
30: Height 19.5cm; Max Width 13.8cm; Thickness 14cm.
31: Height 20cm; Max Width 16cm; Thickness 15cm.

Known as the Cleenish heads these two bulbous heads are thought to have been in the possession of the parish priest of Cleenish at one time.

They are included among the medieval carvings because of their resemblance to the other head from Cleenish (Illustration 29). Their features are carved in a similar manner, oval eyes in false relief, slits for mouths and vaguely defined lips in low relief. All three have oval faces with narrow rounded chins, (one of them broken).

If they are of medieval date these two heads may have belonged to effigial tombs, possibly from St Sinell's Church on Cleenish. A 13th or early 14th century effigy of a knight from Gowran Church, Co Kilkenny, has a similar bulbous head representing a hood of mail. Both Cleenish heads have small shallow sockets at their bases possibly for attaching them to the body of a recumbent effigy. (One of these holes is blocked, the other is only 4.3cm deep and tapers to a point). The tombs, of which they may have formed a part, may now be underneath the military barracks at Enniskillen where so many stones from Cleenish were dumped at the end of the 18th century.

An alternative but less likely suggestion made by Rogers is that they are pagan carvings representing the cult of the severed head.

Hunt, J, *Irish Medieval Figure Sculpture, 1200-1600*, 1974, 2, P1 7.
Rogers, M, *Prospect of Erne*, 1967, 104-105.

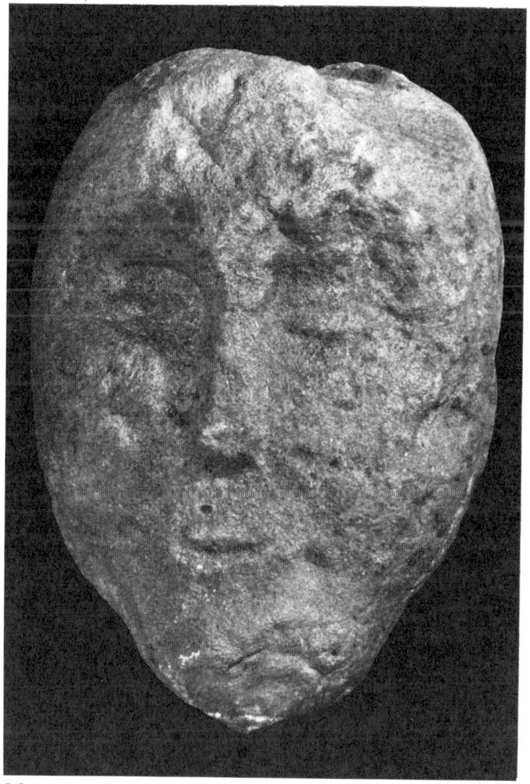
30

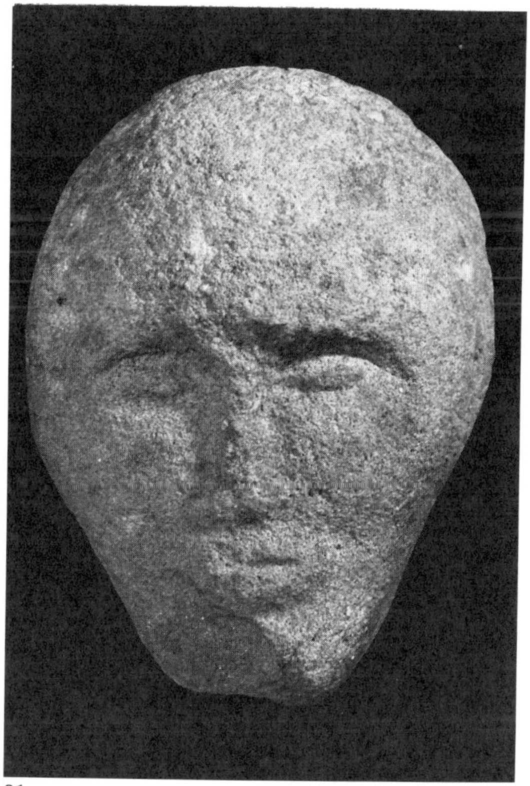
31

32 Decorative Head on Gable-coping (?) from Aghalurcher Church, Fermanagh

Now used as keystone on arch over entrance to graveyard.
Width c. 25cm; Height c. 35cm; Depth c. 75cm.

This stone was possibly the base of a gable coping and belonged almost certainly to the medieval church of St Ronan at Aghalurcher. It may have been used in the restoration of the church in 1447 when the east gable was built and a 'French roof' was erected by Thomas Maguire, Junior ('Annals of Ulster').

The head, which stands out against a concave background, is very weathered. It has a well-defined chin, hollow cheeks and marked hair-line.

Dagg, G A, *J Roy Soc Antiq Ireland*, 1894, 264-270.
Davies, O, *Ulster J Arch*, 1941, 144.
Ancient Monuments of Northern Ireland, 1966, 1, 123.

33-35 Decorative Heads at Drumlane Church, Co Cavan

33: The drip moulding of the fine east window has three head-finials still in position. The two at the sides represent kings, the one on top a bishop. The tracery of the window, of 15th century type, has largely disappeared. The drawing is based on the reconstruction by Oliver Davies.

34: The west door has a weathered bishop's head used as a keystone. The head, which was not part of the doorway originally, may have been a corbel or gable coping in the medieval church (Width c. 14cm; Height c. 23cm; Depth 50cm).

35: Another damaged head has been inserted over the south doorway. It is flat on top and probably was a mask-stop for the drip-moulding of a door or window. It has well modelled stylized ears and a beard represented by diagonally incised lines.

All of these decorative heads and most of the present ruins belonged probably to the medieval church. In the 18th century there were many more heads which have since disappeared. The medieval church was built on the site of an early monastery founded or restored by the 6th century St M'Aodhóg (Mogue or Edan). This became a priory for Augustinian canons probably in the time of St Malachy 1143-8 AD. The present ruins are those of the parish church which apparently existed alongside the priory church. In 1436 an appeal was made for alms to repair both churches.

Davies, O, *J Roy Soc Antiq Ireland*, 1948, 83-94.
Gwynn, A, and Hadcock, R N, *Medieval Religious Houses Ireland*, 1970, 170.

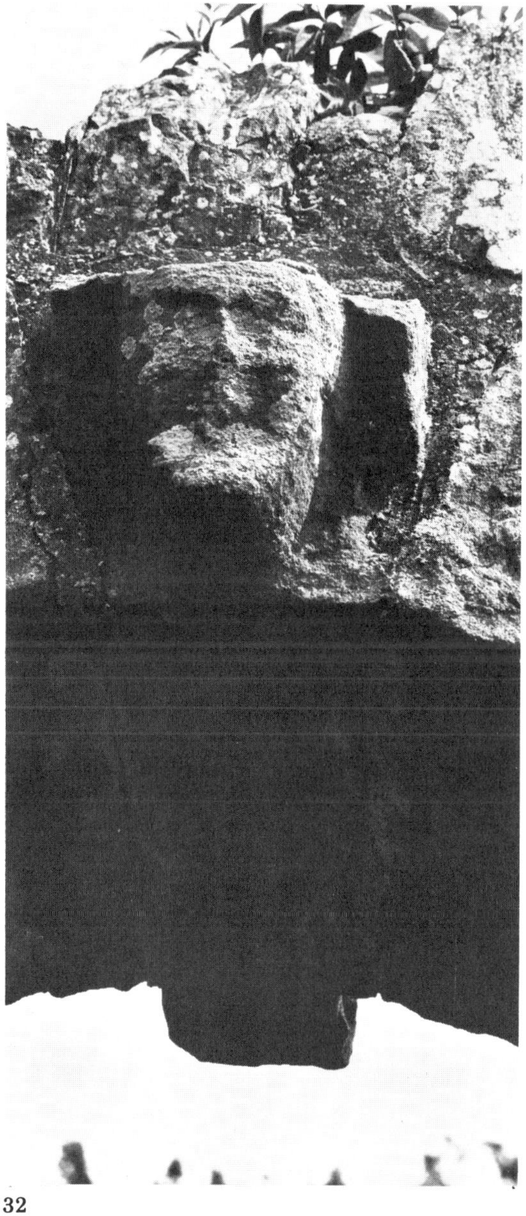
32

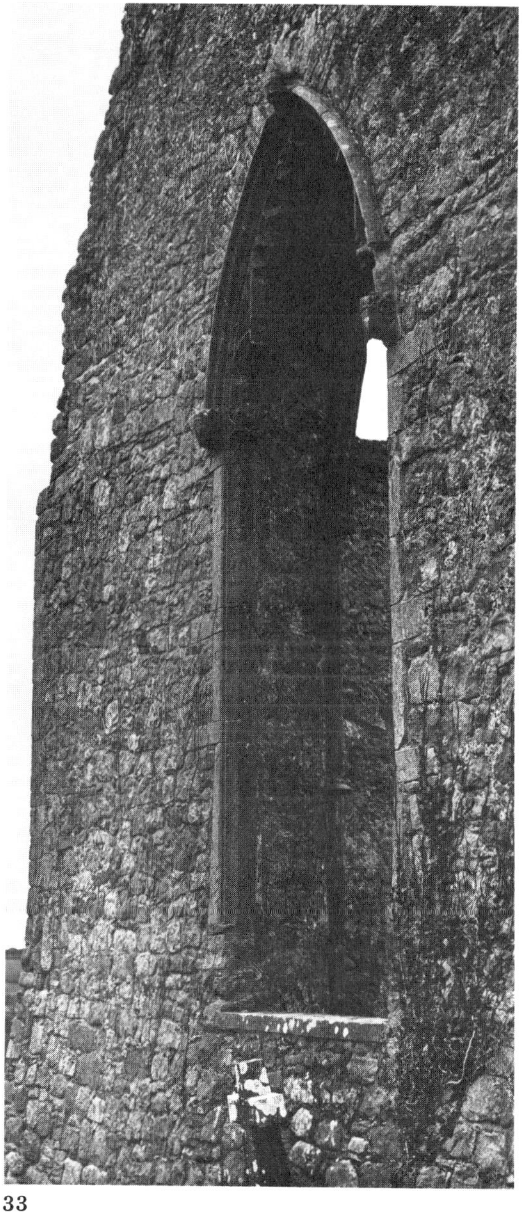
33

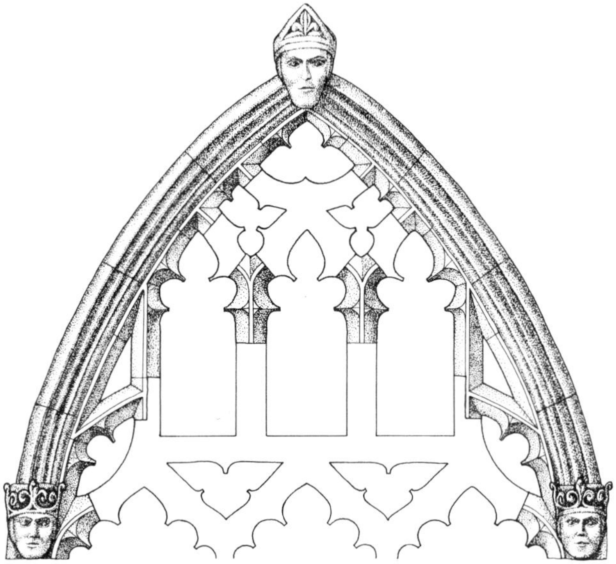
33

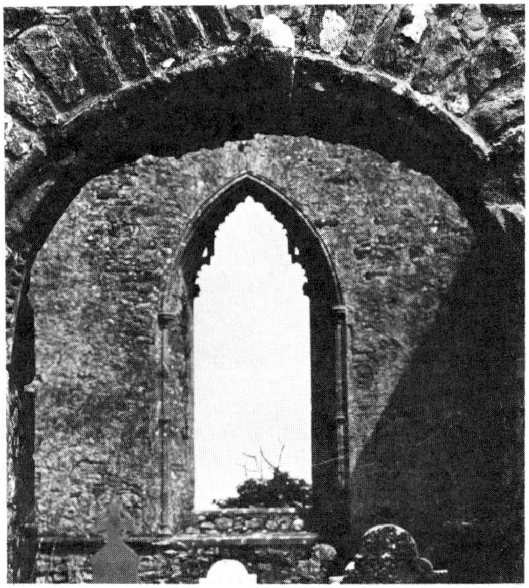
34

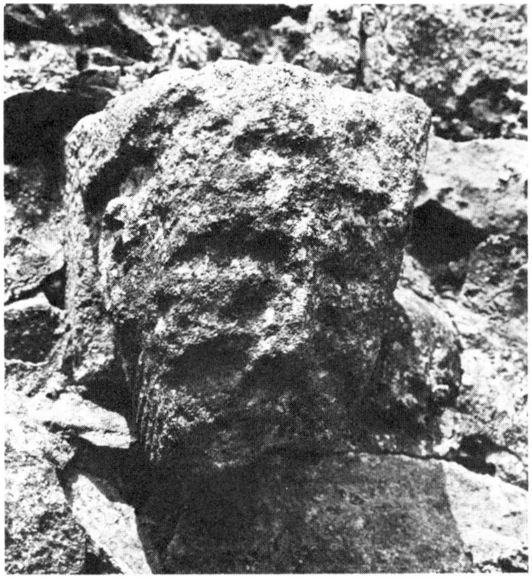
35

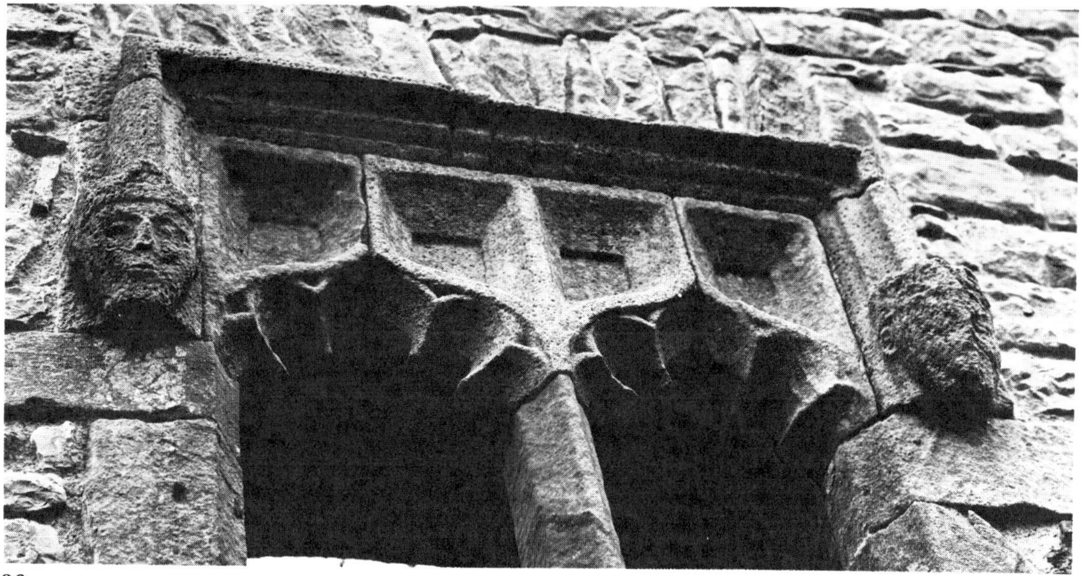
36

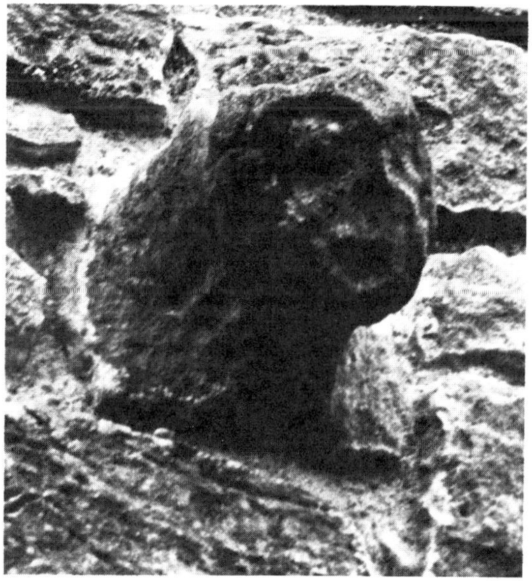
37

36,37 Decorative Heads at Derrybrusk Church (Fyagh townland) Fermanagh

36: The well preserved east window with its twin lights, cinquefoil arch and flat-topped drip moulding provides a good illustration of the use of mask-stops. The two stops are in the form of beautifully modelled male crowned heads. The other carved head (Illustration 37) is set high up at the south end of the east wall and appears to be purely decorative. It is in high relief and has an open-mouthed grotesque face.

37: This was a parish church in medieval times and during the 15th century a guest-house was maintained here. It was the site of an early religious establishment of some kind, perhaps a missionary centre, founded by St Senach who may have been a bishop in the time of St Patrick.

Gwynn, A, and Hadcock, R N, *Medieval Religious Houses Ireland*, 1970, 379.

38 Head from Premonstratensian Abbey, Trinity Island, Lough Oughter, Co Cavan
National Museum Dublin.
Height 21cm; Width 13.5cm; Thickness 13cm.

This small elongated head probably came from the Premonstratensian Abbey and belonged to the 15th century restoration of the church. The abbey was founded, probably in the middle of the 13th century, as a daughter house of the Abbey of Lough Key. The head may have been a mask-stop. It has a very expressive, almost caricaturish face, representing an aged man with a lined face and a furrowed brow.

Davies, O, *J Roy Soc Antiq Ireland*, 1948, 99-100 P1 XIX.

39 Two Unprovenanced Heads in Enniskillen Museum
(A): Height 25cm; Width 20.5cm; Depth 38.5cm. (B): Height 24.5cm; Width 20.7cm; Depth 36cm.

These two very similar heads were given by the late William Steele to the late Lady Dorothy Lowry Corry and were presented to the museum in 1969. They probably belonged to a medieval church, perhaps serving as corbels or mask-stops. Their slight resemblance to Romanesque sculpture may be due to the use of Romanesque models by the medieval stone-carvers. One of the heads (B) has a fresher surface than the other and more obvious tooling marks. It could possibly be a more recent copy of the other. It has been suggested that these heads came from Devenish, Lisgoole or Rossorry but in our present state of knowledge they could just as validly be attributed to any medieval church in the Lough Erne locality.

The two heads differ only in details. The more weathered one has its chin set at a very exaggerated angle unlike that of the other head. Both are wearing what looks like a pill-box type of head-dress but one of these is a plain band in low relief while the other, on the fresher head, is a slightly recessed band marked with vertical striations.

Rogers, M, *Prospect of Erne*, 1967, 134-135.

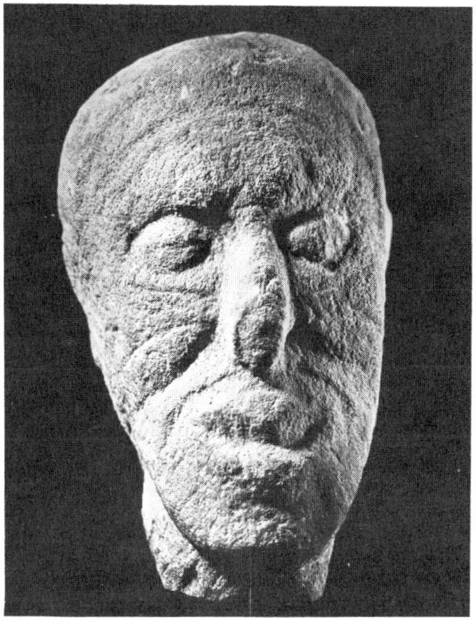
38

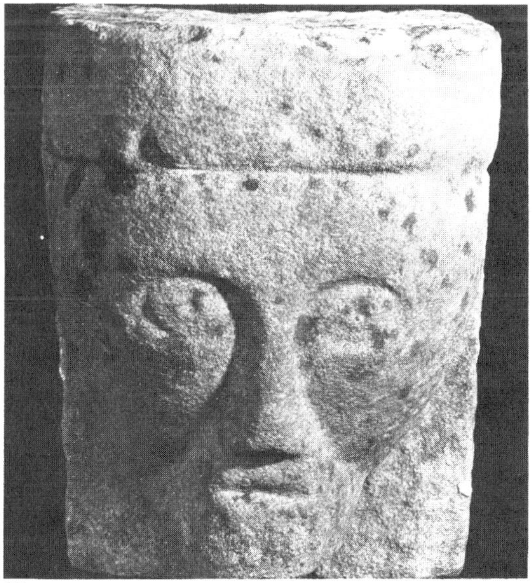
39

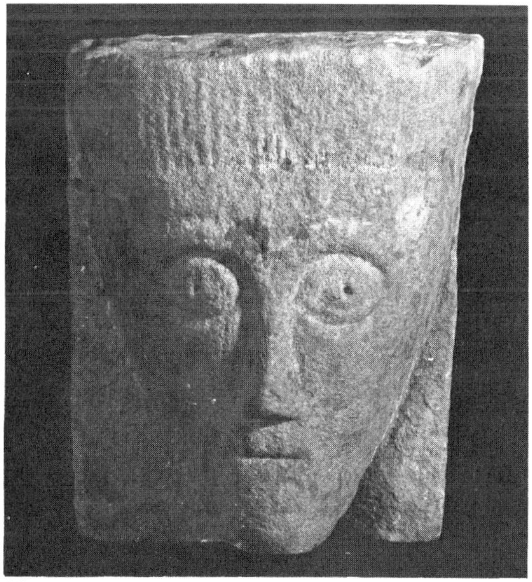
39

40 **Head from Keenaghan Lough beside Tievealough Church, Fermanagh.**
Owned by John Barron, Gadalough, Belleek.
Height 19cm; Max Width 13cm; Max Thickness 22.5cm.

After the water level of Keenaghan Lough had been lowered in 1971 this head was found in the lake close to the south-east shore. This is immediately north of the ruined medieval church of Tievealough. Little is known about this church. It has been described as 'Franciscan' but apparently without much evidence.

The head has a slightly grotesque appearance with round bulbous eyes, wide-open mouth and a beard represented by closely spaced incised lines. It could have been a mask-stop or part of a corbel from the church. At the back of the head is an annular 'collar', half of it shown as a rope moulding, the other half plain, perhaps defaced.

O Gallachair, Rev P, *The Parish of Carn,* 1975, 75.

41 **Head from Castleterra Church, Cavan**
Now above north door of adjoining Roman Catholic Church.

This grotesque head, probably 15th or 16th century in date, is now painted cream to match the colour of the dashed wall in which it is set! It has a very expressive lined face, the furrows forming stylized patterns on cheeks and forehead.

Davies, O, *J Roy Soc Antiq Ireland,* 1948, 80, P1 XI.

42 **Head from Clannaphilip Church in Termon townland, Cavan**
Now set in east wall of sacristy of disused Roman Catholic Church.
Width 6.5cm; Height 20cm; Thickness 14cm.

This grotesque head probably came from the medieval church of Clannaphilip founded by an O'Reilly from Mullagh. The new church beside the sacristy is probably built on the site of this medieval church and graveyard.

This very powerful carving represents a furrowed face, the deeply scored lines being treated in an extremely stylized manner. It may have been a mask-stop. Its strange appearance may have been the reason for it being named locally as the 'Cailleach Gearagain', a local supernatural being supposedly destroyed by St Patrick.

Davies, O, *J Roy Soc Antiq Ireland,* 1948, 98.
Barron, T J, *J Roy Soc Antiq Ireland,* 1941, 133.

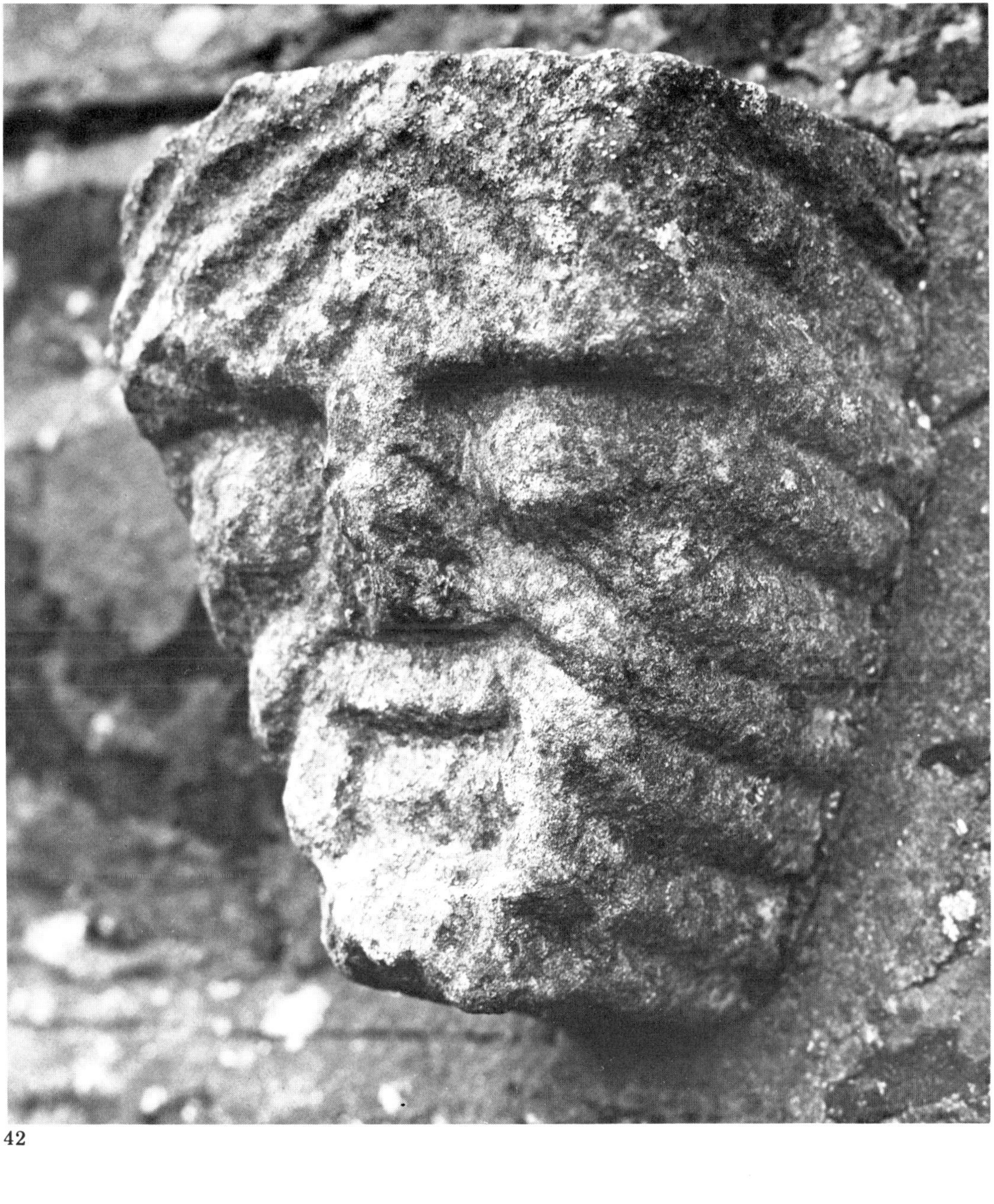

42

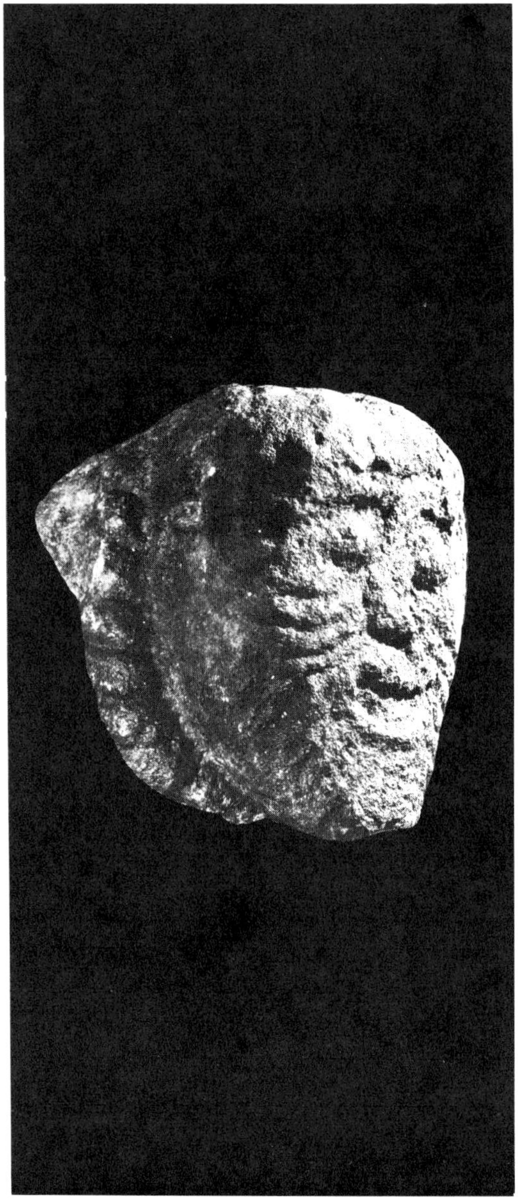
40

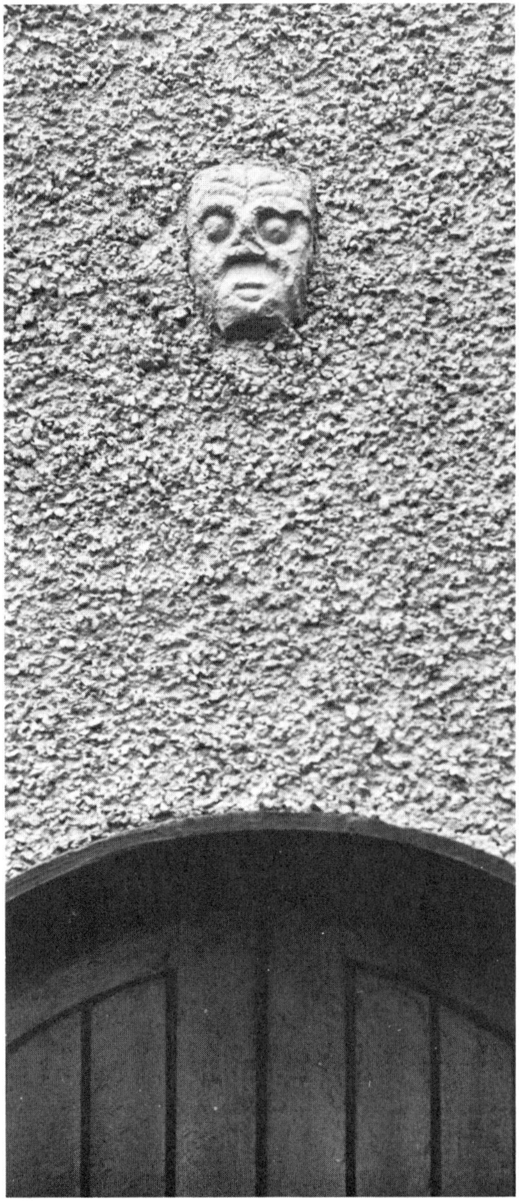
41

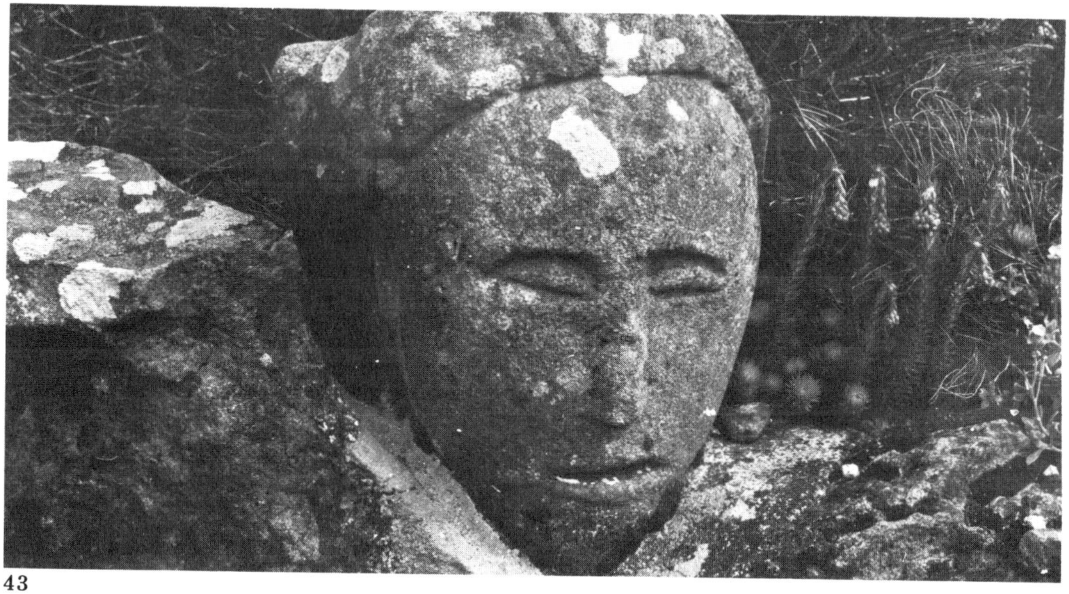

43

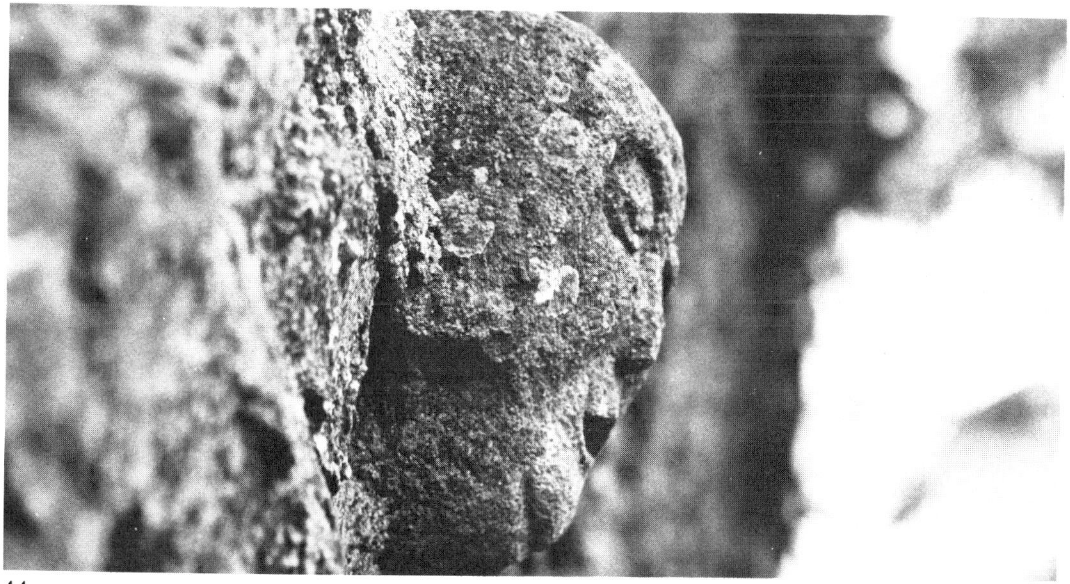

44

43 **Head at Pubble, Fermanagh**
Built into rockery of private house.

This beautifully carved head probably came from the nearby medieval church of Pubble. In the early 17th century the church was also named 'Collidea', which suggests that it originated as a small Culdee monastery (cf Culdees at Killadeas, Illustration 11).

The head is well preserved and was probably a mask-stop. Its slit eyes may represent a dead or sleeping person.

Gwynn, A, and Hadcock, R N, *Medieval Religious Houses Ireland*, 1970, 43.

44 **Head at Derryvullan Church, Fermanagh**
Height c. 25cm.

This head with puffy cheeks, double chin and wavy hair may have been a mask-stop. It probably belonged to the medieval parish church of St Tighernaigh which was built on the site of an Early Christian monastery. The head is now set in the outer cast gable wall of the ruined Protestant parish church which was built in 1776.

Rogers, M, *Prospect of Erne*, 1967, 176-7.

45 **Heads at Drummully Graveyard, Fermanagh**
(A): Width 16.5cm; Height 19cm. (B): Width 15.5cm; Height c. 20cm.
Not illustrated.

Two very weathered heads are now set into the gate-posts at the entrance to Drummully graveyard. They probably belonged to the medieval church (dedicated to St Coman?) some foundations of which survive in the graveyard.

Livingstone, P, *The Fermanagh Story*, 1969, 470.

46 **Head at Carrick Church in Aghamore townland, Fermanagh**

This very weathered head, possibly of a bishop, is the central finial attached to the drip-moulding of the east window. The chin has been broken off and the features are almost totally worn away. This window can be dated towards the end of the 15th century when this church was built by Gilbert O'Flanagan and his wife Margaret Maguire.

47 **Head from Templenaffrin Church, Fermanagh**
Width 20cm; Height 27cm.

This crudely carved head is set in the west gable wall. The face is unusually flat. Round eyes are shown in false relief, the ears are well modelled, the nose is broken and the mouth is no more than a roughly carved slit. The church formerly served as a chapel of ease in the medieval parish of Cleenish. The head is probably not in its original position. It may formerly have been a mask-stop.

Lowry-Corry, Lady D, *Ulster J Arch*, 1938, 25-31.

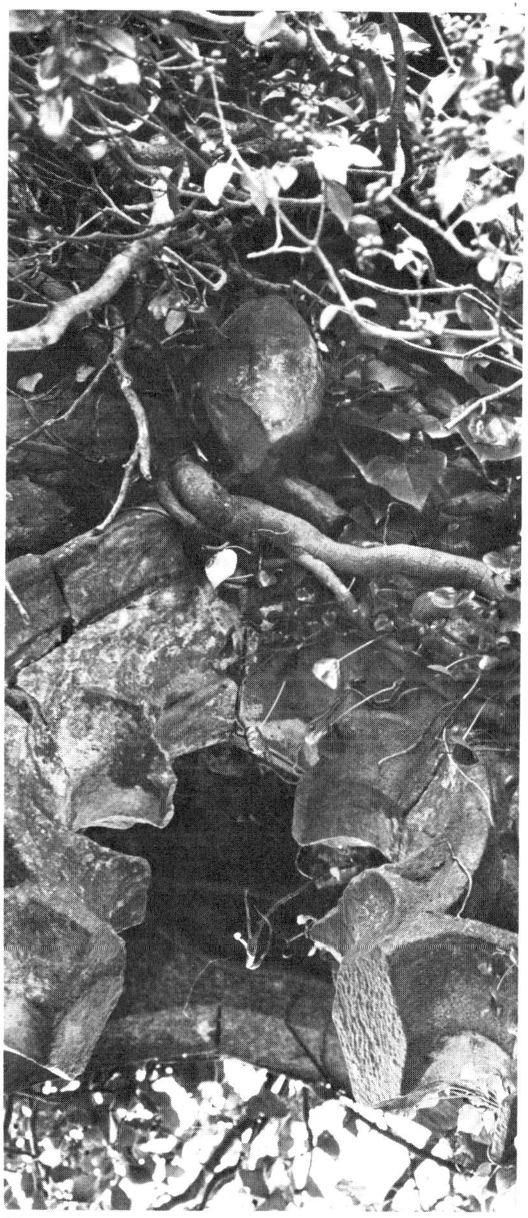
46

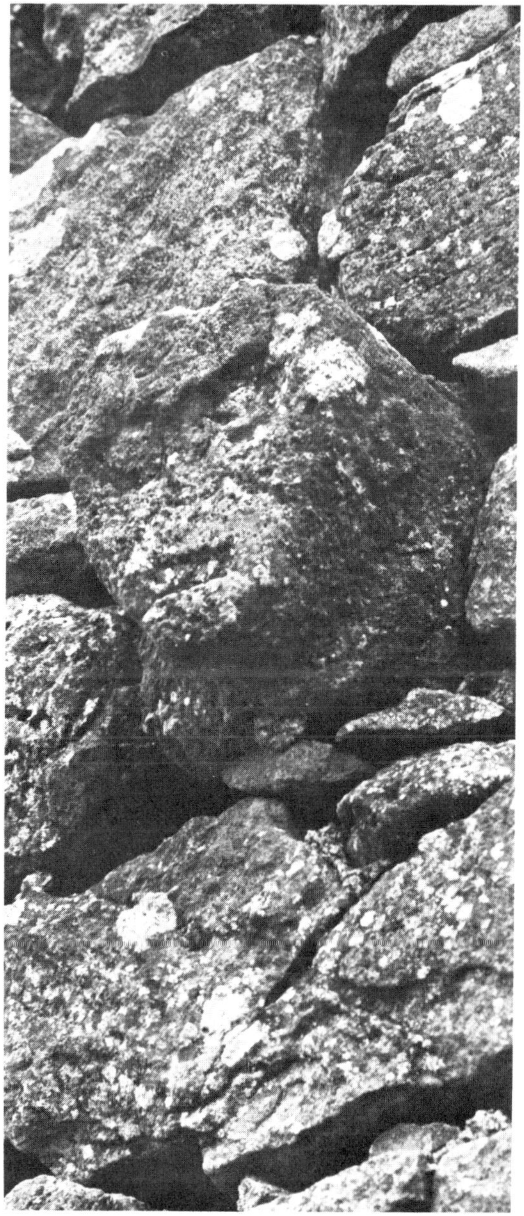
47

48 **Head from farmhouse in Grogey townland, Fermanagh**
Now in Enniskillen Museum.
Width 18cm; Height 23.5cm; Thickness 28cm.

This sandstone head came from a farmhouse which was demolished in Grogey townland, about 3 miles to the east of Brookeborough village. It may originally have been a mask-stop in a church from that locality. It has a broad face with rounded chin. The ears are roughly shaped crescentic protuberances set far back on the head. Traces of red-ochre paint survive on the cheeks, eyebrows and lower lip.

49 **Head at Tempo Manor in Demesne townland, Fermanagh**
Set in wall of outbuilding.

This is one of two heads which formerly decorated the gateposts of Tempo Presbyterian Church. It was rescued by the father of the late Sir John Langham of Tempo Manor when the gateposts were knocked down. The original provenance of this weathered naturalistic head is not known.

50 **Grotesque Female Figure ('Sheila-na-gig') from old church in Cavan (now destroyed)**
National Museum, Dublin.
Width 22cm; Height 43cm; Thickness 12cm.

This very crudely carved female figure is shown in a pose typical of 'Sheila-na-gigs' with widely splayed thighs and with both hands clutching the enlarged open pudenda. The face is particularly distorted with deeply furrowed brow, and the tip of the tongue protruding from a big wide mouth. Beading round the lip probably represents teeth while v-shaped parallel incisions below the chin may indicate ribs.

Guest, E, *J Roy Soc Antiq Ireland*, 1936, 109, P1 IX.

51 **Grotesque Female Figure ('Sheila-na-gig') from Lavey, Co Cavan**
National Museum, Dublin.
Width of Stone 57cm; Height 46cm; Thickness 23cm.

This carving was found about 1842 lying at the entrance to an old graveyard. It probably came from a church within the same graveyard. The figure is shown in a stylized manner with arms extending from cheek level and with legs flexed in a distorted and acrobatic manner. Both hands are clutching the open pudenda shown as a narrow rectangular slot. Underneath the left arm is a discoid object of unknown significance. The eyes are shown as deep holes. This feature and the rough dressing of the stone are strangely reminiscent of the head idol from Tonystick in Fermanagh (Illustration 6) which has been rather tentatively dated to the pre-Christian period.

Guest, E, *J Roy Soc Ant Ireland*, 1936, 109, P1 IX.

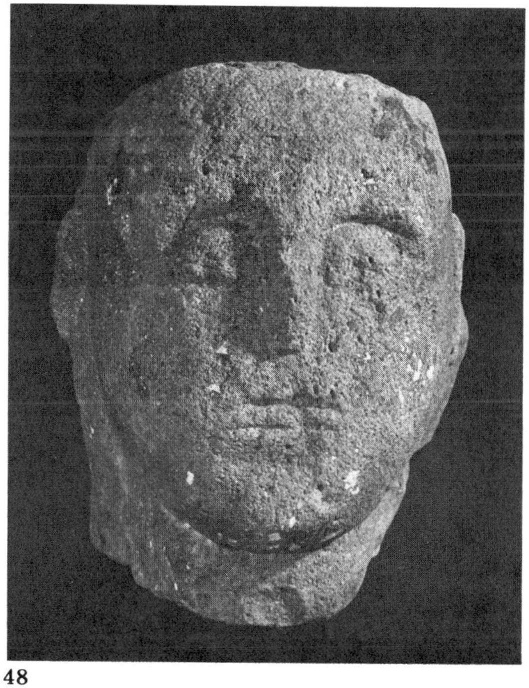

48

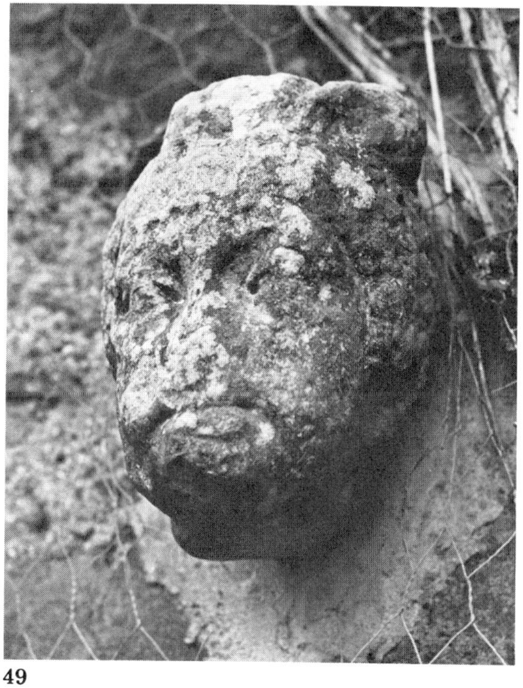

49

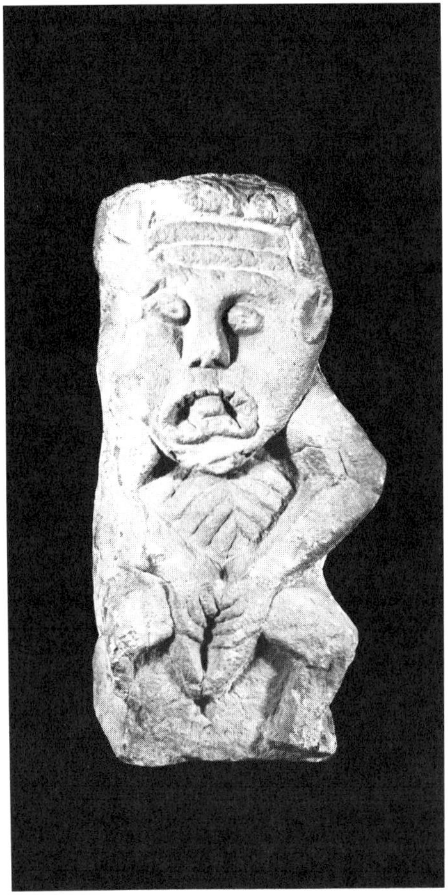
50

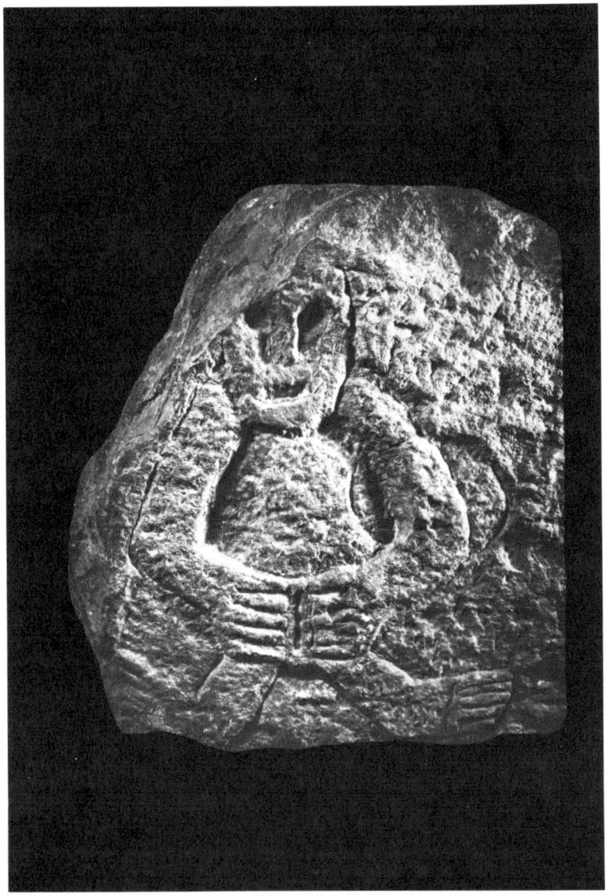
51

Post-Medieval Folk-Art

Heads, Grave-slabs and Busts: 17th to 20th century

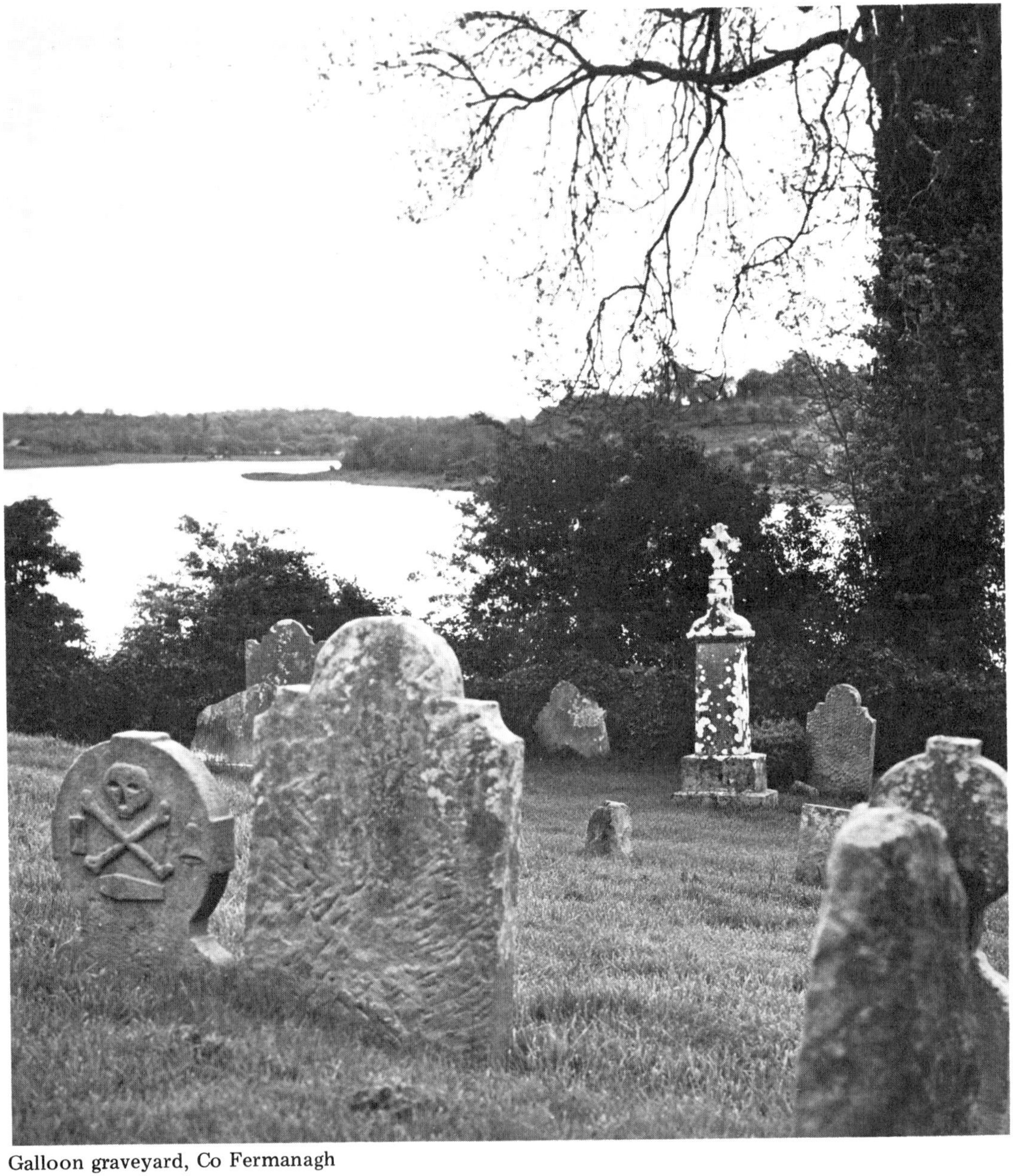

Galloon graveyard, Co Fermanagh

The political and religious upheavals of the 16th and 17th century brought about great changes in the stone-carving traditions of the Lough Erne area. The masons could no longer rely on the customary patronage of the church to maintain their craft. With the dearth of church-building in the 17th century they must have turned their hands to the building of castles for the new settlers, probably assisting master-craftsmen of Scottish origin.

In the early part of the 17th century there was little sign of decorative stone-carving in the Lough Erne area. In the later part of the century the stone-carvers were again employed, this time to make tomb-stones for the new Plantation families. By the second half of the following century tomb-stones were evidently required not just by the Ascendancy but by everyone who could afford to have them made. The Lough Erne stone-carvers responded to this demand with the production of many excellently carved grave-slabs. After Catholic Emancipation in the 19th century church-building received a new impetus and the mason's craft must have been revitalized by the influx of very many English stone-carvers into the country at that time.[1]

Grave-slabs (Illustrations 53-55)

In the east part of Fermanagh, at Pubble, Aghalurcher and Galloon, the stone-carvers produced a very distinctive type of grave-slab bearing the emblems of man's mortality — skull, crossed bones, sand-timer, bell and coffin. (Illustrations 54 and 55). The same emblems are found on earlier recumbent tombstones made for the new Plantation families of this area. Two of these in the vaulted building at Aghalurcher commemorate Elizabeth and James Galbraith who died in 1670 and 1673.[2] The arms of the family are carved at the head of both tomb-stones, the emblems at the base. The latter are carved in relief as are the emblems carved almost a hundred years later on the upright grave-slabs at Aghalurcher. An earlier tomb-stone at Bangor Abbey in Co Down bears the emblems of skull and crossed bones beneath the inscription Memento Mori. It is in memory of another new family, the Bradeshaws and is dated 1620.[3]

The grave-slabs at Devenish are much less remarkable in terms of sculptural image. Large cherubs are carved at the top of the slabs above the inscriptions. The cherub motif is relatively common on 18th and early 19th century grave-slabs. Sometimes it is the only decoration as at Devenish and Killachtee in Donegal. More frequently it is one of numerous motifs as on the elaborately carved grave-slabs from the Leinster area.[4] The Fermanagh grave-slabs are unsigned, unlike the Leinster examples which frequently bear the sculptor's name, often members of the Cullen, Brien and Byrne families. At Devenish in the 1770s there were at least two stone-carvers at work.

Busts

There are five bust carvings in this area, only one of which appears to have had a practical function — the memorial stone from Carnrock (Illustration 61). This may be the work of the same Fermanagh stone-carver who did the very simply carved bust from Belleek (Illustration 59). The remaining three busts come from the area of Derrylin where stone-carving is remembered as a traditional craft of the locality. They are quite remarkable works of sculpture. The strength of their appeal lies both in the simplicity of their form and the vitality which they express.

One of these busts (Illustration 58) is 19th century in date. The uncertain age of the other two busts evokes considerable interest from an archaeological point of view. Are they two hundred years old or perhaps two thousand years old? However this narrow archaeological controversy loses significance in the light of the view expressed by the sculptor Henry Moore that art is 'a universal continuous activity with no separation between past and present'.[5] All these carvings, no matter what their ages may be, express an intense vitality which is common to all good primitive art.

The end of the tradition

The small roughly made concrete head from Blaney (Illustration 62) is a sad illustration of what has happened to the ancient craft of stone-carving. Concrete has come to replace stone as a building material and although there are still a few stone-cutters left in Fermanagh — for example the Mulhollands at Eshbralley — the craft is not being passed on to the next generation. The decline of the craft is lamented in a book of great charm *Stone Mad* written in 1950 by the late Seamus Murphy from Cork, who was himself an exceptionally skilled stone-carver. This remarkable book, in which describes his life among the 'stonies' of Cork, survives as a sort of epitaph to the craft.

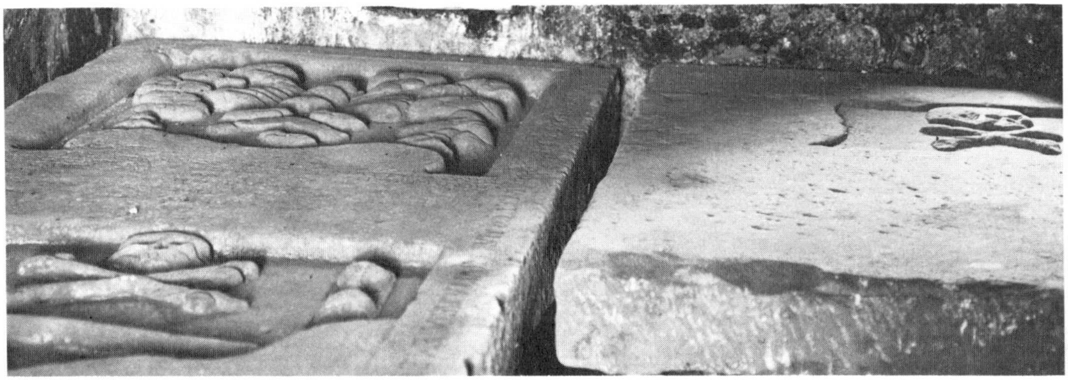

Galbraith tombstone (on left), Aghalurcher, Co Fermanagh

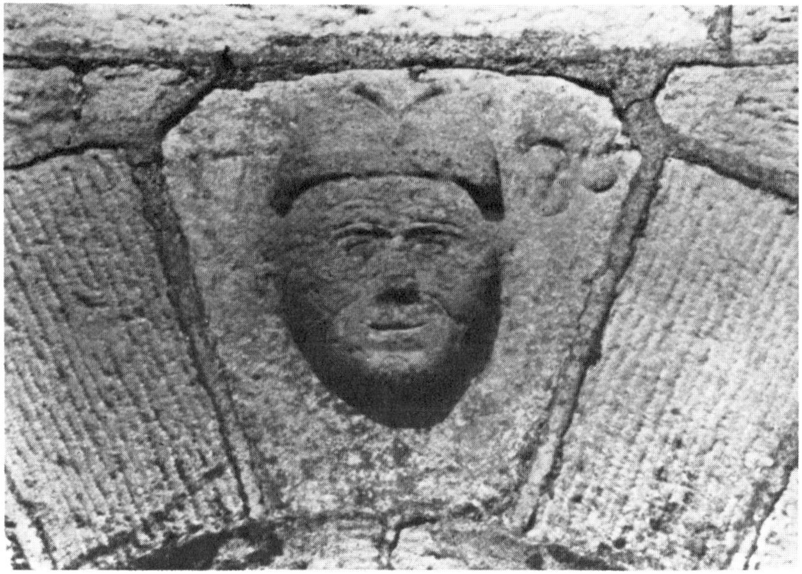
52

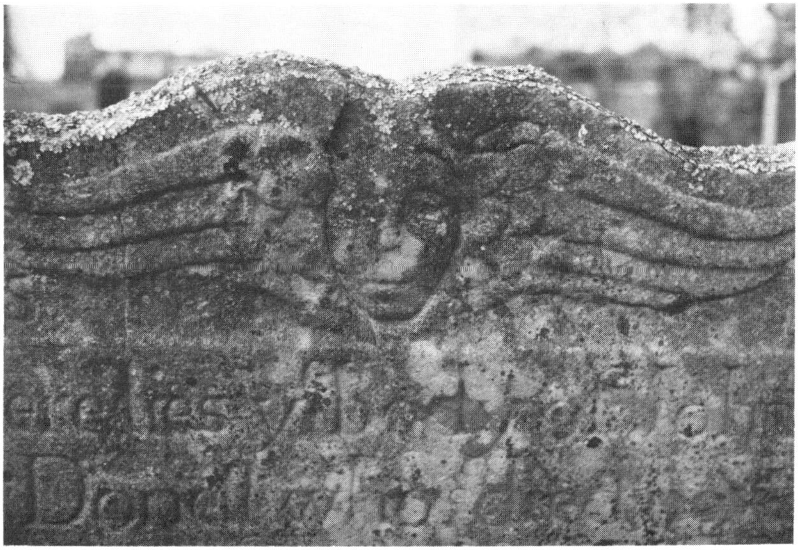
53

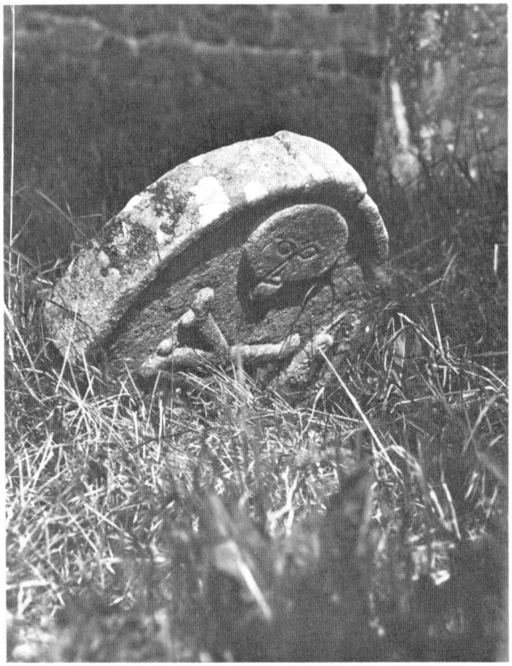
54

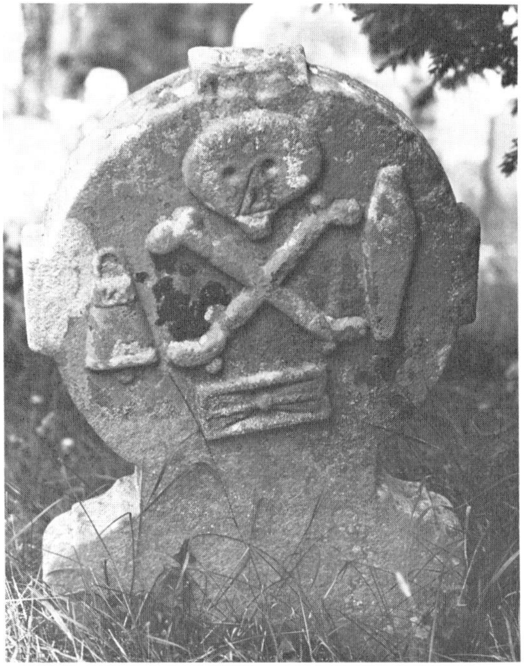
54

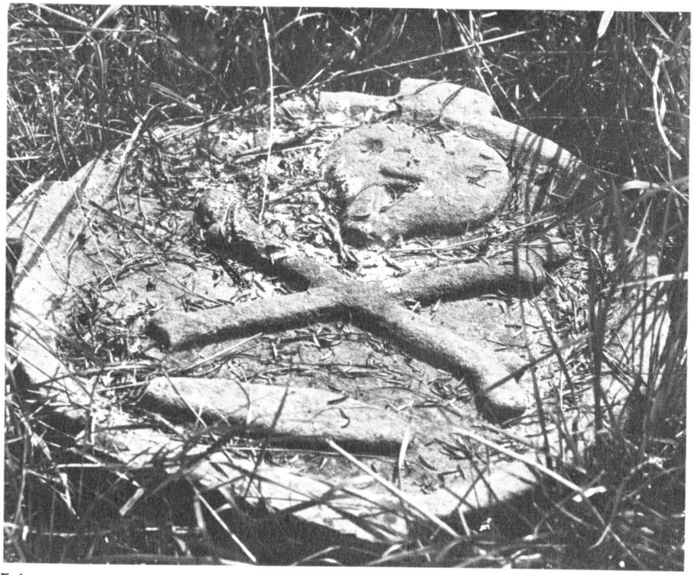

54

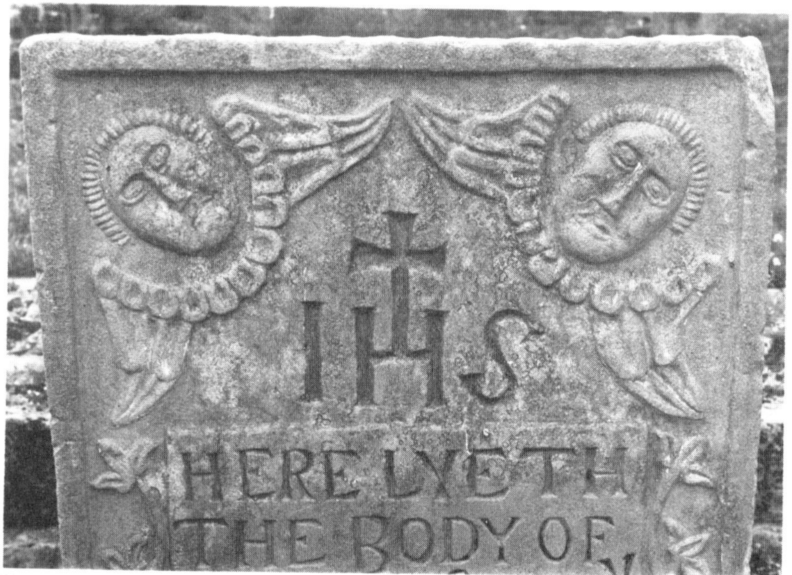

54

52 **Bishop's Head at St Ernan's Church of Ireland Church, Kingscourt, Cavan**

This mitred head, representing St Earnán?, is carved on the keystone over the entrance to the church. It bears the date 1785 which is evidently the date that the present church was built.

The keystone is larger than the other voussoirs of the arch and has a different style of dressing. This could mean that the present arch is later than 1785 and that the keystone was taken from the original archway of 1785. A more likely suggestion is that the date on the keystone is a later addition. The stone may have been brought from the former parish church at Enniskeen, now a ruined building less than a mile to the south-east of Kingscourt. There is some evidence for rebuilding there in the 17th century and this head would not be out of place in such a context.

Davies, O, *J Roy Soc Antiq Ireland*, 1948, 95-96.

53 **Grave slabs at St Molaise's church Teampul Mor, Devenish Island, Fermanagh**

54 **18th century grave slabs from Aghalurcher, Co Fermanagh**

55 **18th century grave slabs from Galloon, Co Fermanagh**

56 **Male Bust from Mullyneeny townland, Derrylin, Fermanagh**
Height 57cm; Width 43cm.

This impressive carving now stands in a somewhat undignified position on top of an old septic tank beside the former RUC barracks in Derrylin. Formerly it was set among farm buildings to the rear of the barracks.

It has an unusually severe hair-line falling to below ear-level. The oval eyes are slightly convex and the lips and rounded jaws are well modelled. Neck and shoulders are indicated by a gradually splaying base. The bust now presents a strange, distorted appearance on account of damage to its nose and old paint adhering to its surface. A black moustache has been painted on to it. Cheeks are painted pink, hair and eyebrows a deep black.

It is very difficult to date this carving. It is probably a work of folk-art belonging to the 18th or 19th century, a forerunner to the bust by Maguire in Derrylin (Illustration 58). But it could be much earlier, perhaps even pre-Christian. It has a marked ridge between the shoulders and the narrow vertical band at the base of the bust. This band may originally have been designed to allow the bust to fit neatly into the socket of a plinth. Because of the indeterminate age of this bust it is of interest to note that the same kind of base occurs on a very small two-faced 'Celtic' idol from Leichlingen in Germany where the ridge has been interpreted as a torc and the idol dated to the 4th century BC.

Megaw, J V S, *Art of the European Iron Age*, 1970, 81, P1 85.

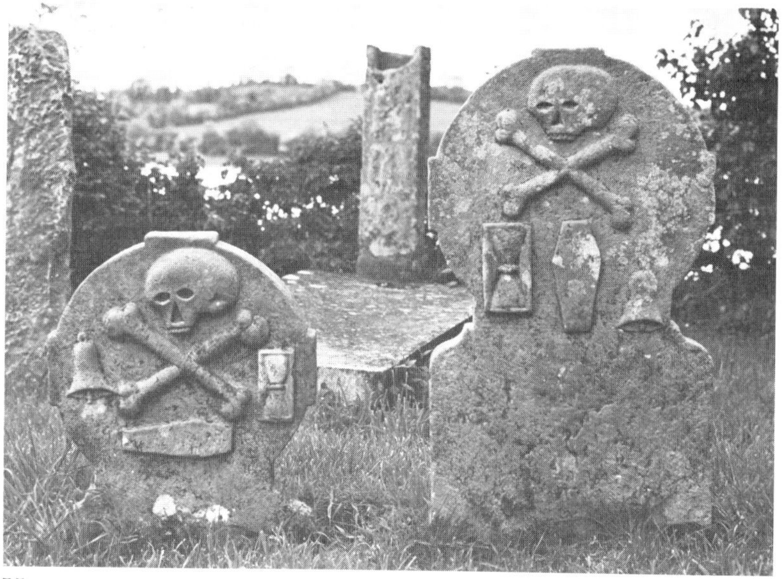

55

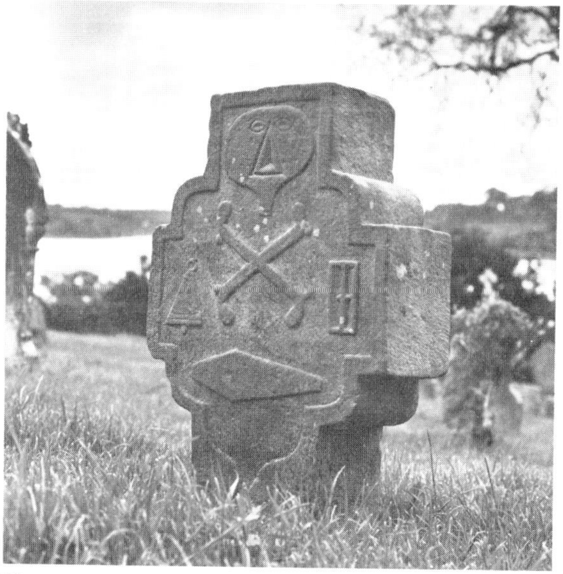

55

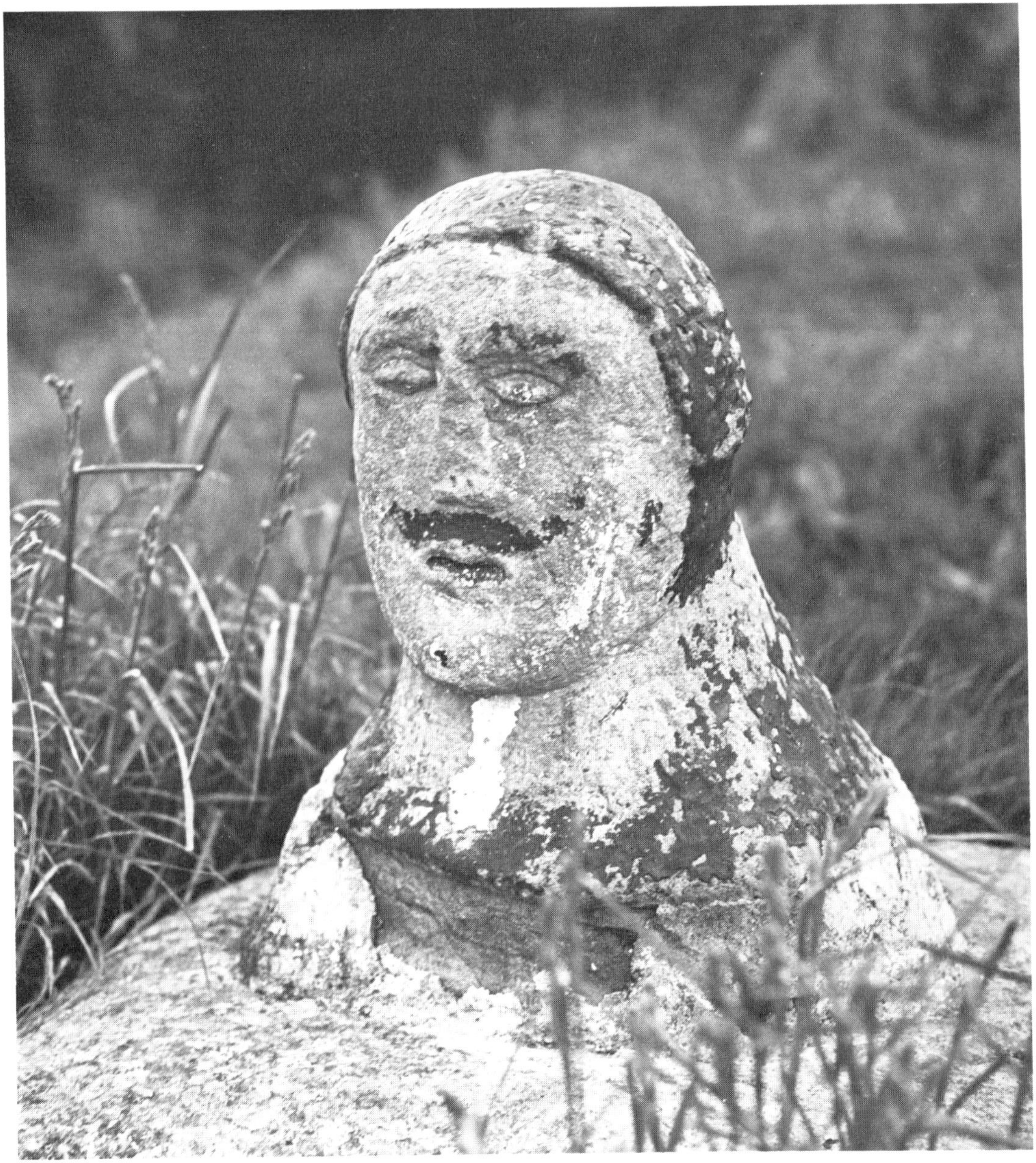

56

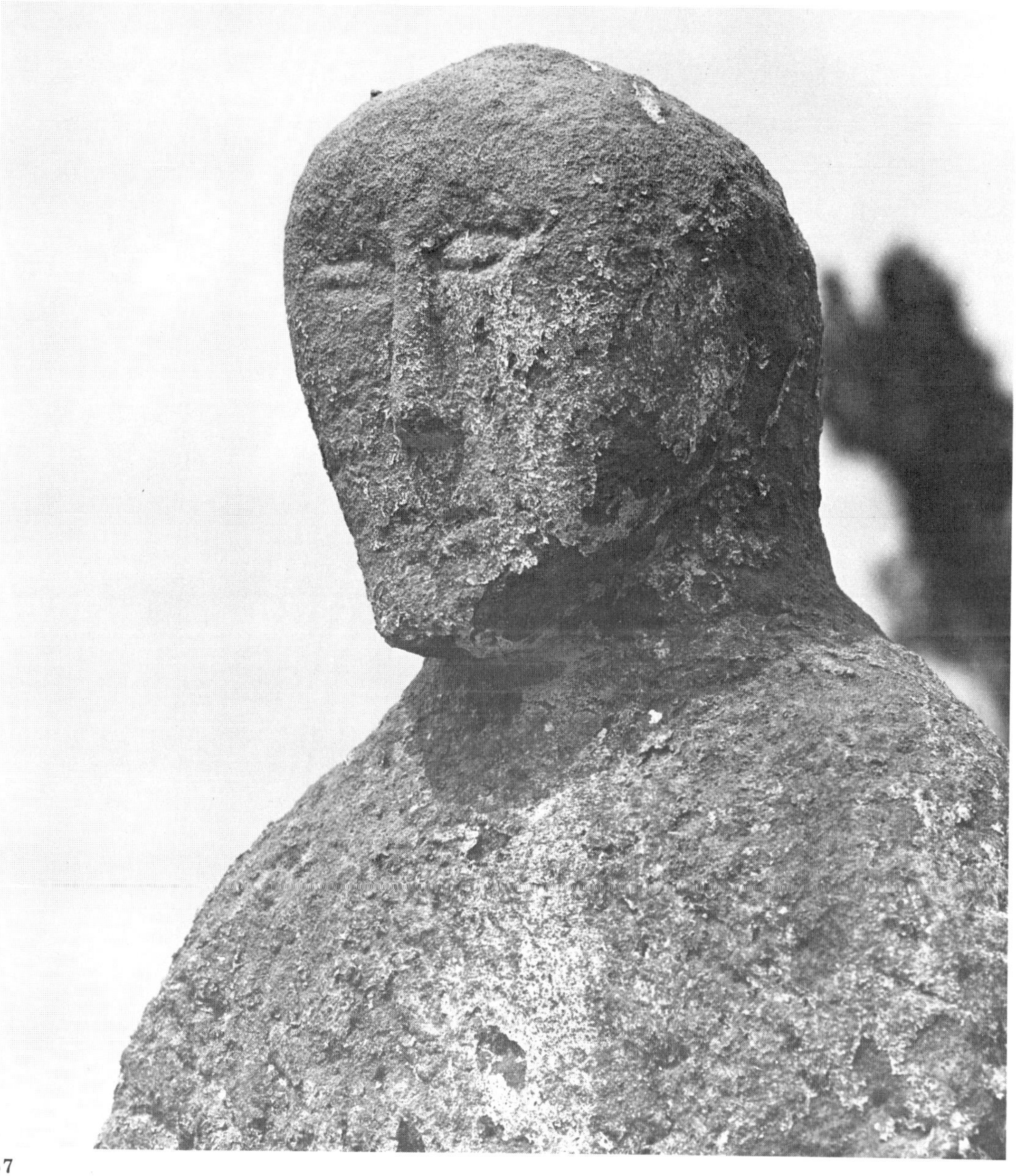

57

57 **Male Bust from Callowhill townland, near Derrylin, Fermanagh**
On gate-pier beside Surphlis' house.
Height 59cm; Width 46cm; Depth 25.5cm.

Formerly this was set on top of an archway which once spanned the avenue to the nearby house. It is not known whether or not this was its original position. Nor is there any certainty about its age.

The head leans slightly forward and the form of the thick neck and rounded shoulders is suggested rather than clearly defined. A noteworthy characteristic of this bust is that apart from the well-moulded wedge-shaped nose, the surface of both face and chest is extremely flat. The mouth is a mere slit, the eyes two simple oval shapes. Many of its features are similar in style to those of the 19th century bust from Derrylin (Illustration 58) — the well-formed nose, close-set eyes, slit mouth and flat cheeks.

58 **Male Bust from Derrylin, Fermanagh**
Beside Blake's Public House.
Height 65cm; Width 59cm; Depth 20cm.

This was carved by a local stone-mason named Maguire about the middle of the last century. Formerly it stood on the other side of Blake's Public House next to what was then a Masonic Lodge. At that time it was known locally as 'King Billy'.

Dramatically painted in black and white, the figure is clad in a lapelled coat and bow tie. It has well carved eyebrows, a cleft chin and very stylized hair resembling the rolls of a wig. Its other features are similar to those on the nearby Callowhill bust (Illustration 57) — a wedge-shaped nose, close-set eyes, slit mouth and flat cheeks. A line of black paint serves as a moustache.

59 **Male (?) Bust from Belleek, Fermanagh**
Height c. 30cm.

This crudely carved bust survives beside the ruins of Slater's Public House. It is believed to have been the work of a local stone-carver in the third quarter of the 19th century. The face has a slightly concave surface, a small prim mouth and big startled eyes.

Rogers, M, *Prospect of Erne*, 1967, 161.

60 **Bishop's Head from Carneyhill, Arney, Fermanagh**
Owned by Charles Cassidy, Carneyhill.
Height 23cm; Width 15cm; Depth 15cm.

This head may not be from either Cavan or Fermanagh. It was formerly owned by the father of the present owner who lived in Sessiagh townland, Arney, but who had been stationed in other parts of the country while working with the Royal Irish Constabulary.

The head supports a mitre with double peak. The face is bearded, the ears are well modelled and the mouth is shown as a straight slit. Its nose has been broken. The presence of carefully carved hair at the back of this head suggests that, unlike medieval mask-stops, it was designed to be free-standing. It is probably the head of a statue.

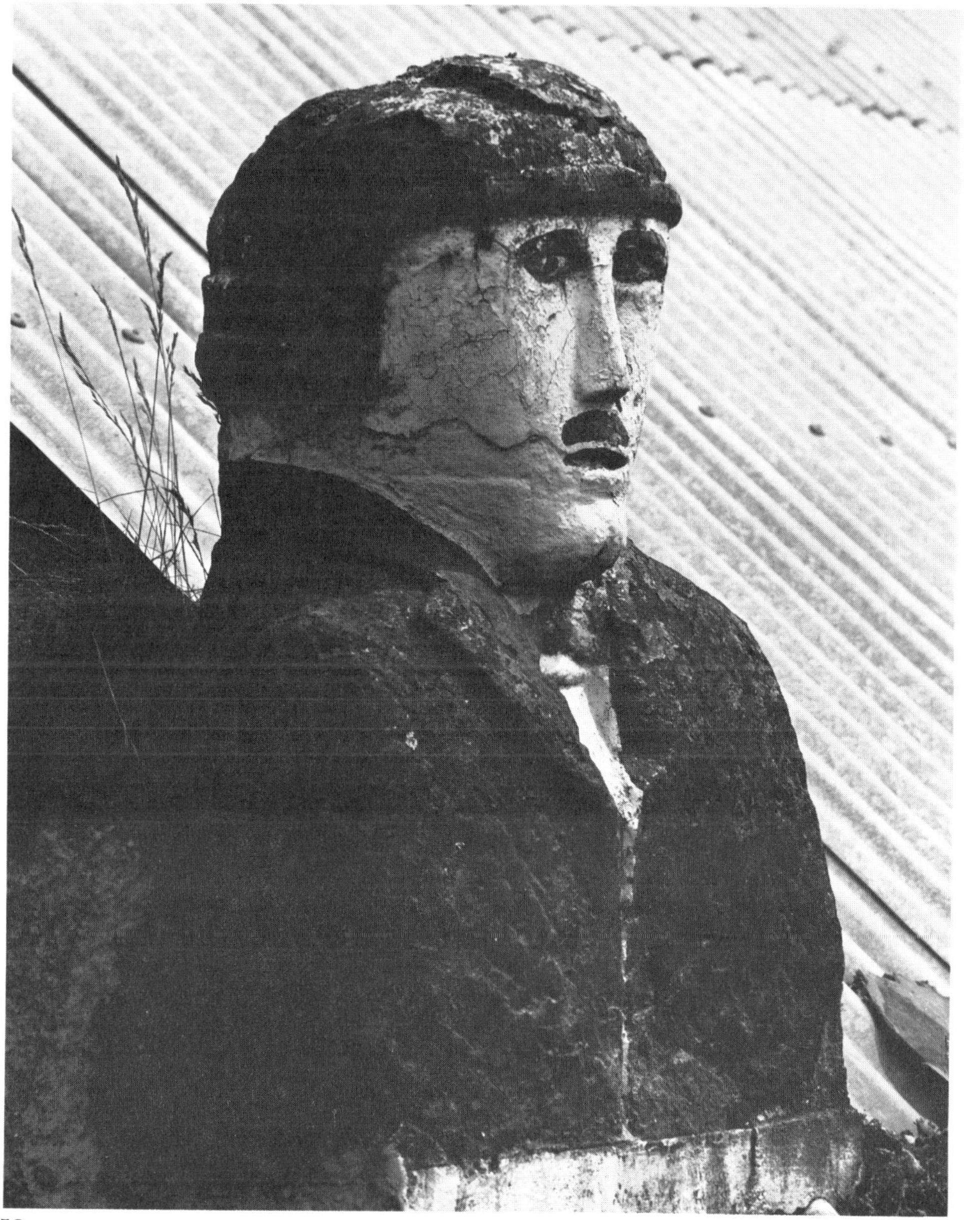

58

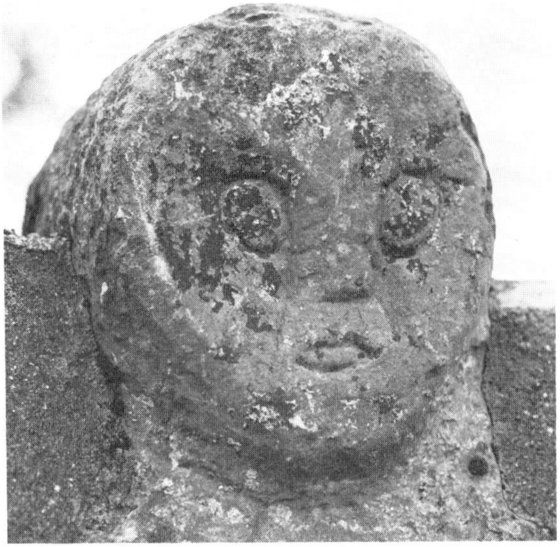
59

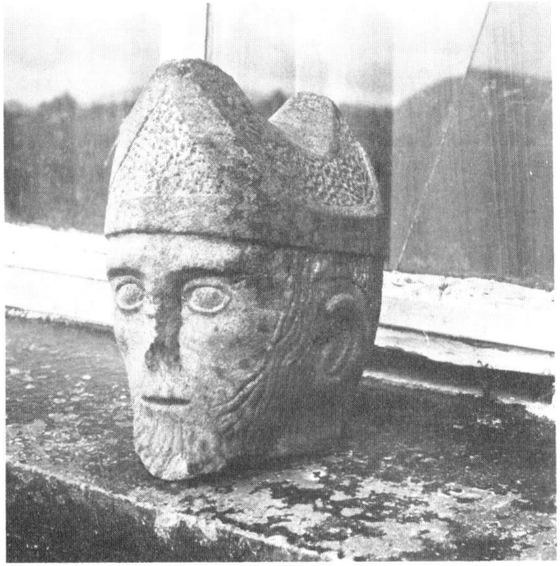
60

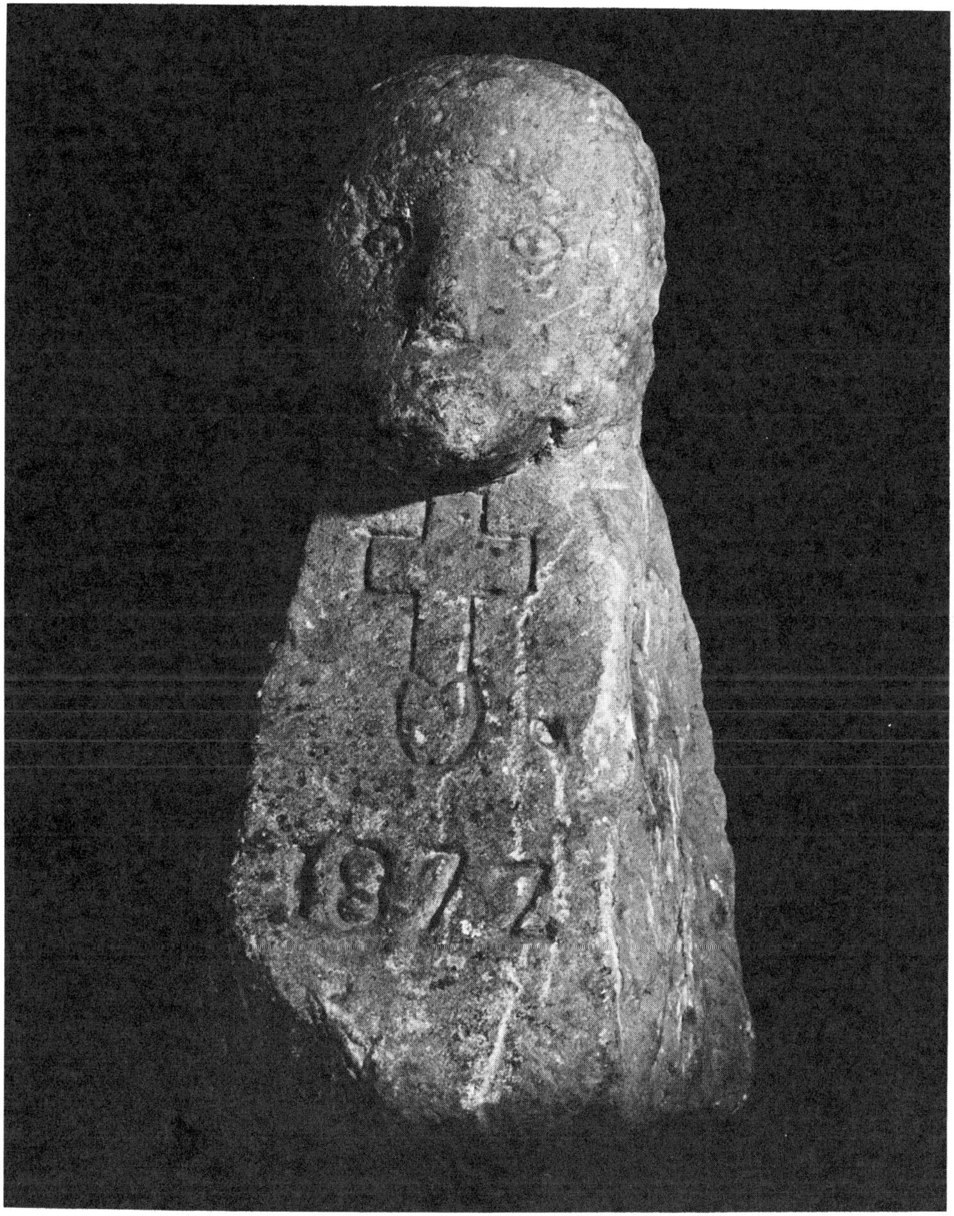

61

61 **Female (?) Bust, Carnrock, Fermanagh**
Now in Cassidy's Folk Museum in Lisnaskea.
Height 44cm; Width 26cm; Thickness (at base) 30cm.

This sandstone bust consists of a simply carved face, not unlike that of the Belleek bust (Illustration 59) above a flat panel which bears an incised cross and the date 1872. It is believed to be a memorial to Judy Flanagan, member of a local family, who died in 1872. The cross is a simple outlined cross with a heart-shaped base. The features are simplified — small near-circular shapes for eyes, a mere slit for a mouth. The nose and part of the pointed chin are broken and only the front of the stone has been dressed.

62 **Concrete Head from Blaney, Fermanagh**
Owned by Mr and Mrs Ritchie, Old Mill House, Blaney.
Height 15cm; Width 10.5cm; Depth c. 12cm.

Despite its obvious modernity with its brass-ringed base and hair ornament of broken china, this head retains the same kind of power and vitality so characteristic of earlier folk-art from this area. Indeed, had it been made of stone one might have accepted it as being a much older work. It is simply and rather crudely made. The face is smooth and the hair is made of very coarse concrete. The facial expression is severe. The mouth is a mere slit, the eyes two small deep holes. Traces of silver paint still adhere to its surface.

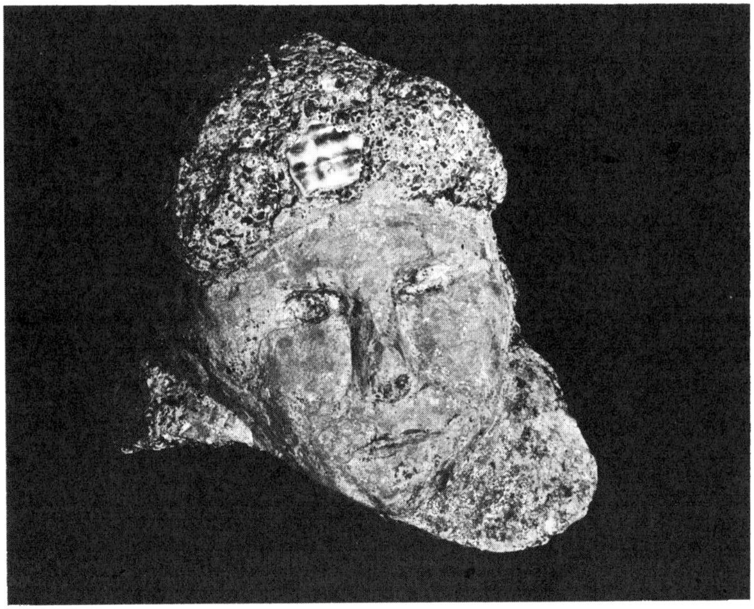

62

Maps

Idols of the 'Celtic Religion 3rd century BC to 5th century AD

1 Head Idol, Corravilla, Cavan
2 Head Idol, near Cavan town
3 Double figure, Dreenan townland, Boa Island, Fermanagh
4 Three-faced Head, Corleck or Drumeague, Cavan
5 Head from Janiform carving, Corraghy, Cavan
6 Head Idol from Tonystick townland, Enniskillen
7 Carved Deity from Lustymore Island, Fermanagh
8 Wooden Idol, Ralaghan, Near Shercock, Cavan

Christianity: Statues and High Crosses 9th-11th century AD

9 Shaft of High Cross, Inishkeen Island, Fermanagh [Detail of Head]
10 Shaft of High Cross, Toneel graveyard, Boho, Fermanagh
11 Shaft of East Cross, Galloon Island, Fermanagh
12 Shaft of West Cross, Galloon Island, Fermanagh
13 Shaft of High Cross, Lisnaskea, Fermanagh [Adam and Eve]
14 Six Statues from White Island, Lower Lough Erne, Fermanagh
15 Carved Head on White Island, Lower Lough Erne, Fermanagh
16 Carved Pillar ('Bishop's Stone') Killadeas graveyard, Fermanagh

Romanesque Figure Carving 12th century AD

17 Carved Heads on Cornice of Round Tower, Devenish Island, Fermanagh
18 Romanesque Doorway from Trinity Island, Lough Oughter, Cavan
19 Male Exhibitionist Figure on Romanesque Window, Berrymount, Cavan
20 Male Exhibitionist Figure on Gable-coping or Cornice, Aghalurcher, Fermanagh
21 Figure of Bishop at Aghalurcher Church, Fermanagh

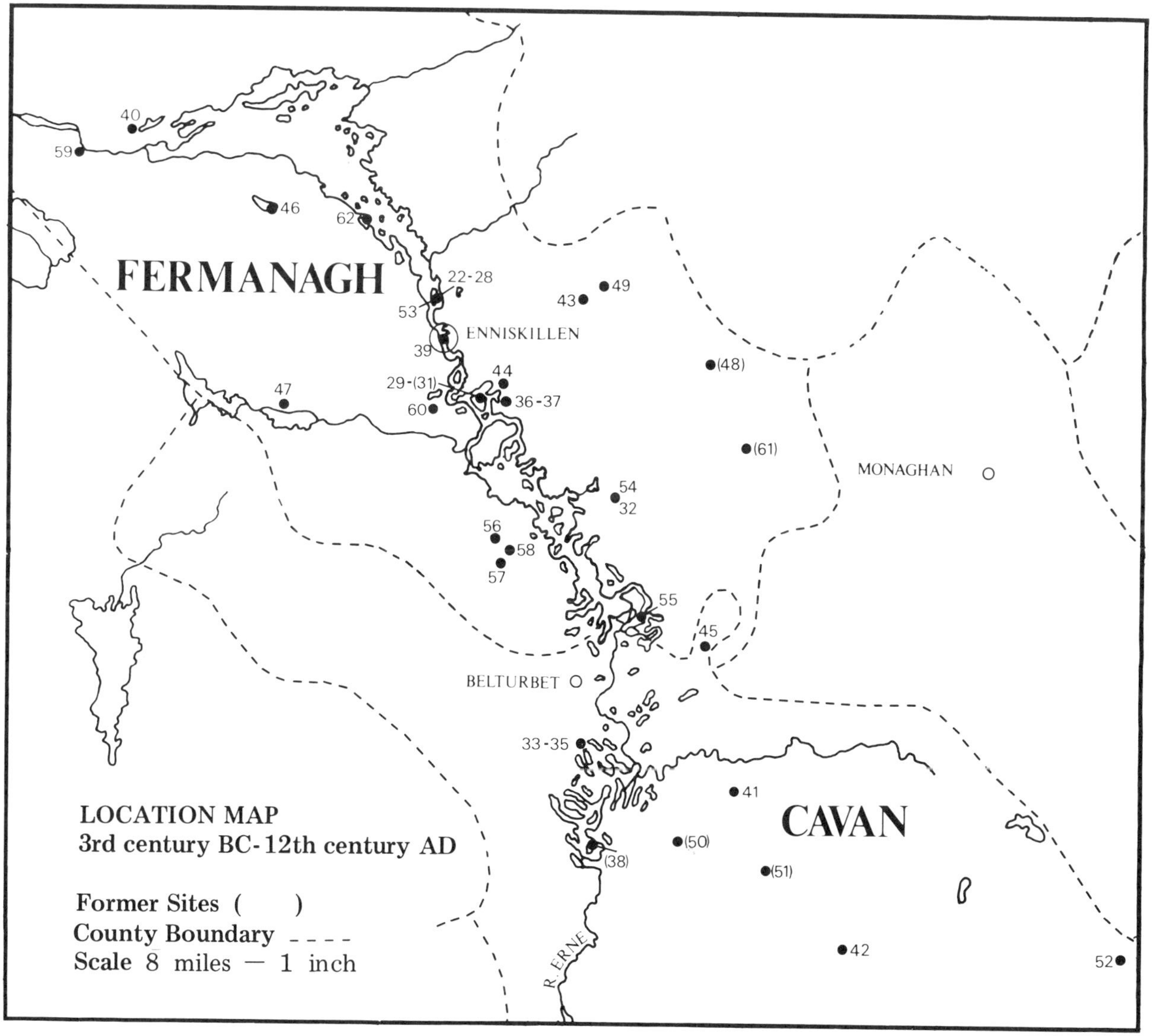
FERMANAGH
CAVAN
ENNISKILLEN
MONAGHAN
BELTURBET
R. ERNE
40
59
46
62
22-28
53
39
43
49
(48)
44
29-(31)
36-37
60
47
(61)
54
32
56
58
57
55
45
33-35
41
(50)
(38)
(51)
42
52
LOCATION MAP
3rd century BC-12th century AD
Former Sites ( )
County Boundary
Scale 8 miles — 1 inch

The Medieval Period: Decorative Heads and other Carvings from Medieval Churches 13th-16th century

22 Grotesque Head from St Molaise's Church (?) Devenish Island, Fermanagh
23 Bishop's Head at St Mary's Augustinian Priory, Devenish Island
24 Coffin Lid from Graveyard of St Mary's Augustinian Priory, Devenish Island
25 Grotesque Head in site-museum Devenish Island
26 Cross-slab at St Mary's Augustinian Priory, Devenish Island
27 Head-finial from west door of St Mary's Augustinian Priory, Devenish Island
28 High Cross in graveyard of St Mary's Augustinian Priory, Devenish Island
29 Decorative Head on Gable-coping from church on Cleenish Island, Fermanagh
30,31 Two Heads possibly from Cleenish Island
32 Decorative Head on Gable-coping (?) from Aghalurcher Church, Fermanagh
33-35 Decorative Heads at Drumlane Church, Cavan
36,37 Decorative Heads at Derrybrusk Church (Fyagh townland), Fermanagh
38 Head from Premonstratensian Abbey, Trinity Island, L. Oughter, Cavan
39 Two Unprovenanced Heads in Enniskillen Museum
40 Head from Keenaghan Lough beside Tievealough Church, Fermanagh
41 Head from Castleterra Church, Cavan
42 Head from Clannaphilip Church in Termon townland, Cavan
43 Head at Pubble, Fermanagh
44 Head at Derryvullan Church, Fermanagh
45 Heads at Drummully Graveyard, Fermanagh
46 Head at Carrick Church in Aghamore townland, Fermanagh
47 Head from Templenaffrin Church, Fermanagh
48 Head from farmhouse in Grogey townland, Fermanagh
49 Head at Tempo Manor in Demesne townland, Fermanagh
50 Grotesque Female Figure from old church in Cavan
51 Grotesque Female Figure from Lavey, Cavan

Post-Medieval Folk-art; Heads, Grave-slabs, Busts 17th-20th century AD

52 Bishop's Head at St Ernan's Church of Ireland Church, Kingscourt, Cavan
53 Grave-slabs at St Molaise's Church (Teampul Mor) Devenish Island, Fermanagh
54 Grave-slabs in Aghalurcher Graveyard, Fermanagh
55 Grave-slabs in Galloon Graveyard, Fermanagh
56 Male Bust from Mullyneeny, Derrylin, Fermanagh
57 Male Bust from Callowhill, near Derrylin Fermanagh
58 Male Bust from Derrylin, Fermanagh
59 Male (?) Bust from Belleek, Fermanagh
60 Bishop's Head from Carneyhill, Arney, Fermanagh
61 Female (?) Bust, Carnrock, Fermanagh
62 Concrete Head from Blaney, Fermanagh

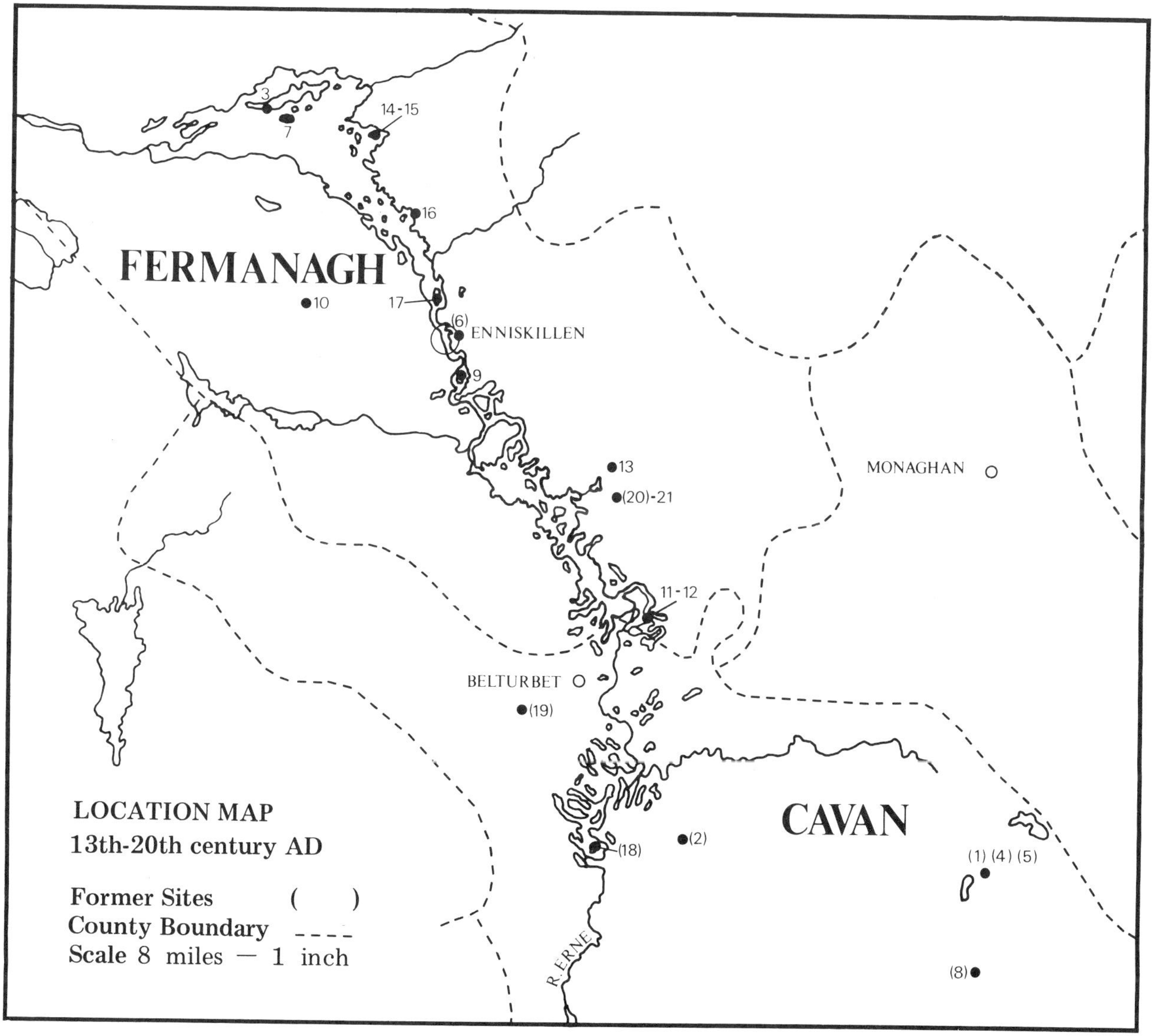
FERMANAGH
CAVAN
MONAGHAN
ENNISKILLEN
BELTURBET
R. ERNE
3
7
14-15
16
10
17
(6)
9
13
(20)-21
11-12
(19)
(18)
(2)
(1) (4) (5)
(8)
LOCATION MAP
13th-20th century AD
Former Sites ( )
County Boundary
Scale 8 miles — 1 inch

References

Introduction

1 Henry, F, *Irish Art during the Viking Invasions*, 800-1020 AD, 1967, 193.
2 Henry, F, and Zarnecki, G, *British Archaeol Assoc J*, 1957-58, 31.
3 Richardson, Rev J, *The Great Folly of Pilgrimages in Ireland*, 1727, 68.
4 Greene, K T, *Antiquaries J*, 55(2) 1975, 338-345.
5 Touring Exhibition arranged for the Arts Council of Northern Ireland , Autumn 1976.

Chapter 1

1 Dillon, M, *Celts and Aryans*, 1975, 20-21
2 Ross, A, *Pagan Celtic Britain*, 1967, 62.
3 Piggot, S, *The Druids*, 1968, 56.
4 Ibid, 57.
5 Megaw, J V S, *Art of the European Iron Age*, 1970, 78, Pl 76.
6 Ross, A, op cit, 66, 271.
7 *Annals of Ulster 1185 AD*
8 Dillon, M, op cit, 29.
9 MacNeill, M, *The Festival of Lughnasa*, 1962, 8.
10 Dillon, M, op cit, 30.
11 Ross, A, op cit, 92-93.
12 Ibid, 78-79.
13 Lambrechts, P, *Contributions a L'Etude des Divinités Celtiques*, 1942, 40.
14 Megaw, J V S, op cit, Pl 12.
15 Lambrechts, P, op cit, 21-26, 161.
16 Rynne, E, *C B A Research Report*, 9, 1972, 86; Sandford, E, *Discover Northern Ireland*, 1976, 141.
17 Rynne, E, op cit, 86.
18 Esperandieu, E, *Recueil général des bas-reliefs, statues et bustes de la Gaule romaine*, 5, 1913, 8, no 3655.
19 Ross, A, op cit, 73-74.
20 Lambrechts, P, op cit, 160-161.
21 Ibid, 40.
22 Rynne, E, op cit, 83; Jackson, S, *Celtic and other Stone Heads*, 1973, 34.
23 Barron, T, *Clogher Record*, 1976, 98-102.
24 Ross, A, op cit, 343.
25 Jackson, S, op cit, 31.
26 MacNeill, M, op cit, 172.
27 Ross, A, in *The Witch Figure* (edited V Newall) 1973, 144, 157.
28 Rogers, M, *Prospect of Erne*, 1967, 81.
29 Prendergast, E, *Old Kilkenny Review*, 17, 1965, 49-52.
30 Piggott, S, op cit, 86.
31 MacNeill, M, op cit, 171-72.

Chapter 2

1 Ó Duígeannáin, M, in *Essays and Studies presented to Professor Eoin MacNeill* (ed J Ryan), 1940, 296-306.
2 Ettlinger, E, *Ogam*, 10, 1958, 265-272.
3 Sharkey, J, *Celtic Mysteries, The Ancient Religion*, 1975, 22.
4 Henry, F, *Irish Art during the Viking Invasions*, 1967, 192.
5 Smith, W, and Cheetham, S, (ed) *A Dictionary of Christian Antiquities*, 1875, 73.
6 Cabrol and Leclercq, *Dictionnaire D'Archeologie Chrétienne*, 1924, 1346.
7 Smith, W, and Cheetham, S, (ed) op cit, 73.
8 Brawnfels, W, *Monasteries of Western Europe*, 1972, 38-39, 45.
9 Macalister, J, *Roy Soc Ant Ireland*, 68, 1938, 298-300.
10 Waterman, D W, *Ulster J Arch*, 1959, 65-66.
11 De Brefny, B, and Mott, G, *The Churches and Abbeys of Ireland*, 1976, 8-10.
12 Macalister, J, op cit, 298-300.
13 Cole, J H, *J Cork Hist and Arch Soc*, 1907, 61.
14 Henry, F, op cit, 140.

Chapter 3

1 Clapham, A W, *Romanesque Architecture in Western Europe*, 1936, 21-22.
2 Henry, F, *Irish Art in the Romanesque Period 1020-1170 AD*, 1970, 155.
3 Henry, F, and Zarnecki, G, *British Arch Assoc J*, 20-21, 1957-58, Pl IV and V.
4 Henry, F, and Zarnecki, G, op cit, 17.
5 Henry, F, *Proc Roy Irish Acad*, 61, 1960-61, 37.
6 I am grateful to Anthony Weir for this information, for much helpful discussion about exhibitionist figures and for referring me to some useful publications about the subject.
7 Hutchinson, G E, and A L, *Proc Isle of Wight Natur Hist Archaeol Soc*, 6(4) 1969, 247, Pl 2(a).
8 Ross, A, in *The Witch Figure* (ed V Newall), 1973, 148.

Chapter 4

1 Simms, K, *The Medieval Kingdom of Loch Erne*, unpublished lecture 1-2.
2 Livingstone, P, *The Fermanagh Story*, 1969, 40-42.
3 Stop or mask-stop = projecting stone in the shape of a human head or face at the ends of a hood or drip moulding.
4 Corbel = a stone projecting to support something over it.
5 Gable coping = top course of masonry in gable wall.
6 Sharkey, J, *Celtic Mysteries, The Ancient Religion*, 1975, 8.
7 O'Rahilly, C, (ed) *Táin Bó Cúalnge*, 1970, 170-171.
8 Hutchinson, G E, and A L, *Proc Isle of Wight Natur Hist Archaeol Soc*, 6(4), 1969, 247.

Chapter 5

1 Murphy, S, *Stone Mad*, 1966, 5.
2 Maguire, N, *Clogher Record*, 2, 1957, 334-5.
3 Bigger, F J, and Hughes, H, *Ulster J Arch* 1900, 196-7.
4 Longfield, A, *J Roy Soc Antiq Ireland*, in vols from 1943 to 1947 inclusive.
5 Moore, H, *Henry Moore on Sculpture*, 1966.